new dimensions in jazz guitar

by
REZ ABBASI

AF009565

In loving memory of Lon M. Teller, Paul La Rose, and Ahmad Mansour

Speed • Pitch • Balance • Loop

To access audio visit:
www.halleonard.com/mylibrary

Enter Code
1118-0727-5837-4279

ISBN: 978-1-4950-3615-6

Copyright © 2018 by HAL LEONARD LLC
International Copyright Secured All Rights Reserved

No part of this publication may be reproduced in any form or by
any means without the prior written permission of the Publisher.

Visit Hal Leonard Online at
www.halleonard.com

Contact Us:
Hal Leonard
7777 West Bluemound Road
Milwaukee, WI 53213
Email: info@halleonard.com

In Europe contact:
Hal Leonard Europe Limited
Distribution Centre, Newmarket Road
Bury St Edmunds, Suffolk, IP33 3YB
Email: info@halleonardeurope.com

In Australia contact:
Hal Leonard Australia Pty. Ltd.
4 Lentara Court
Cheltenham, Victoria, 3192 Australia
Email: info@halleonard.com.au

CONTENTS

5 PREFACE

6 INTRODUCTION
- 6   Flow
- 6   Space
- 7   The Board

8 CONNECTION
- 8   Phrasing
- 10   Staccato Picking
- 10   Consecutive Skipping
- 11   Long Tones

12 EXPANDING EMOTIONAL AWARENESS
- 12   A Different Mindset
- 12   Melody Without Harmony
- 13   Emotion-to-Scale Ratio
- 14   Giving Voice to the Instrument
- 14   Nine Emotions (Navarasa)

16 GAINING CONTROL
- 16   THE FIVE COMPONENTS
- 16   1. Melody
- 18   2. Harmony
- 24   3. Rhythm
- 33   4. Technique (muscle development)
- 34   5. Tension

51 EXPANDING THE BOARD
- 51   Horizontal Engagement

54 DISCOVERY MIRROR (exercises for revealing deficiencies)
- 54   Navigation Skills (for horizontal playing)
- 54   Tune in a Box (vertical)
- 55   The Four Horsemen

56 COMPOSITIONAL PLAYING
- 56   Call/Response/Echo
- 58   Character
- 60   Compositional Variation and Applications

62 BREAKING OUT OF HABITUAL PLAYING
- 62   Playing Standards in Odd Meters
- 62   Start on the Opposite Beat
- 62   Doubling Notes
- 62   Replace Any Note
- 62   Employ Compositional Variation
- 63   Launch Phrases
- 63   Varying Line Length
- 63   Chain-Linking (nonstop eighth notes)
- 63   Left-Hand Combinations

64 PRACTICE METHODS
- 64   Shock Practicing
- 65   Soloing Alone (with a bass player in mind)
- 65   Soloing Alone (with a drummer in mind)
- 65   Using the Television

66 IDEAS TO CONSIDER
- 66   Technique vs. Vocabulary
- 66   Timing vs. Targeting
- 68   Tools vs. End Result
- 68   Hearing/Feeling vs. Thinking/Calculating

69 JAZZ AND AWARENESS

71 RECOMMENDED BOOKS

71 ACKNOWLEDGMENTS

71 ABOUT THE AUTHOR

72 DISCOGRAPHY

PREFACE

For some, playing an instrument comes naturally, but for others, it can be more challenging. The outcome of good music-making has little to do with talent, however, and more to do with what one practices and how one thinks. Wherever one lies on the spectrum of "natural ability" is secondary. With a solid and systematic approach to the guitar, along with hard work, anyone can see tremendous and long-term improvement.

The musical and philosophical collection of ideas in this book have been brewing for decades through my own experiences and research. I've harvested them through working with a variety of great instrumentalists, vocalists, dancers, students, teachers, and from the process of overcoming my own array of obstacles. Through rigorous years of troubleshooting, I have reached a place in my development that gives me reason to write this book. Many of the ideas and exercises are "homegrown."

Having control generates freedom.

The content in this book is geared towards direct and specific application. Here, you will not see endless pages of scales, arpeggios, chord voicings, or licks because there are many books (some good) containing those requisite nuts and bolts, and presenting material of such a nature would be redundant. This book is directed towards guitarists who already have the essential nuts and bolts under their belt and are now looking to expand into places they have perhaps not thought about.

Furthermore, there is no emphasis on any specific style or a specific way of playing; instead, this is a resource of information that will help the player gain more control over the guitar by stimulating new physical and emotional pathways.

INTRODUCTION

FLOW

Several potent, extra-musical analogies can be applied to how we approach playing the guitar. One such analogy lies in racing off-road motorcycles, better known as "motocross." Years ago, I read an interview of a world champion motocross racer speaking about the most effective way to approach riding any given track. He referred to a mindset, saying that, while riding, thinking "through" the track, rather than on "top" of the track, made a significant difference; riding on "top" of the loose dirt, moguls, and jumps will hamper the timing of the ride because your focus is placed on the separate elements confronting you at each moment. Conversely, riding "through" the track will help you evaluate the bigger picture, allowing you to focus on the flow of the ride. Certainly, all elements need to be considered, but the point I took away from his advice, and the way in which I found it applicable to music, is that one needs to be cognizant of how a potentially meaningful outcome can easily be undermined by less significant details.

We can see how this analogy might apply to improvising with the guitar. Like the motocross track, the guitar presents myriad obstacles that have the potential to hinder a good outcome. As guitarists, in order to get to the point that allows us to play "through" the instrument on a high level, we need to remove all obstacles. On the contrary, if we are continually dealing with separate elements while performing (e.g., fingerings, scales, technique, weak rhythm, or poor reading skills when needed), we will not be able to create the desired flow that comes from a broader bird's-eye view.

Try the following exercise, as it may give you a clearer understanding. Open a fakebook and choose a complex tune that you are *unfamiliar* with. Look it over for only a minute, scanning for any potential pitfalls. Then begin playing a solo while taking note of the difference between playing on "top" versus playing "through." On "top" would mean you are stopping and starting, trying to figure out what scales fit with which chords, which arpeggio or fingering works in a given area, which notes are common tones between chords, etc. In other words, connecting with the separate "tools" but not with the music. In this sense, you are forced to focus on the jumps, turns, and loose sand but not on winning the race (or, in our case, making music).

In contrast, when playing through an area of the tune that feels more comfortable, you will notice a natural flow. The difference can be fairly obvious, and once you feel that difference, it will serve as a gauge to help you become more aware of when you are playing the guitar through any piece of music, as opposed to on top.

Prior to a motocross race, professional riders take a few warmup laps in order to study the characteristics of the track (in our case, a new piece of music). By this time in the rider's career, he is already trained to grasp 80 percent of any given track and simply needs to get a feel for the new "changes." Due diligence serves him well, as he does not need to get off his bike and check each turn, each jump, or each set of bumps (scales, chords, arpeggios, fingerings, etc.), as these have been dealt with in prior practice. He now moves not on top but through the track, placing his attention on flow (music).

SPACE

As a longtime fan of boxing, I've learned a lot about the sweet science of the sport by way of analysis from trainers, boxers, and through the media. What is apparent is that the elite boxers are the ones who make a statement not only with their fists or offense but also with their defense. They make use of the entire ring to create space between them and their opponent, which ultimately enables them to influence the outcome of the fight. On the contrary, I've often seen exceptionally talented fighters lose fights because they have lacked good defense: they end up bull-rushing their opponent, smothering their own ability to land strong, well-timed punches. They often rely too much on knockout power as a means to an end. Mike Tyson, the great heavyweight, finally lost to boxers who had some of the offensive goods he possessed but were more in control of themselves defensively and therefore more in control of the outcome. The consistently greatest fighters engage from a conscious balance of offense and defense.

I like to view the use of defense in boxing as akin to using breath or space in music. Employing breath as part of a solo is often overlooked because it's not something technical that we have worked on—a new idea, rhythm, etc. Our natural tendency is to become overzealous with ideas, which ultimately smothers the band with content. Applying even a little space between some of our ideas allows us, the soloist, a moment to focus on what we have previously stated and what might be stated next. Importantly, it also allows the band to communicate within our phraseology, which then provides us with new information to solo from—it's a win-win situation.

> *"When you solo, make the drummer sound good."*
>
> —Thelonious Monk

Luckily, we don't have to contend with someone using us as a punching bag; however, if you play with certain types of drummers in jazz, it can feel like a boxing match—never knowing when to expect a jab or power punch. We can react to these events (accents) in two ways: 1) keep throwing punches back with the hope that something will synch up (land), or 2) use a little space, which will allow us to "utilize the entire ring" and make more effective musical choices; and when things do synch up, it will be more meaningful. Of course, there is a time for both, and only you can decide what is best.

THE BOARD

Decades ago, I stumbled upon a magazine called *Psychology Today*. The feature article was on chess, and even though I'm not a chess player myself, there was something that stuck. The author conducted a study based on the mindset of elite chess champions. He concluded that players of that ilk have the ability to view the entire board at once. Any move their opponent makes will be overshadowed by their own perception of the board. The elite player can literally see many moves ahead of their opponent.

How is this analogous to guitar playing? All guitar players know the fingerboard is also a complex matrix, rendering endless possible combinations, and the better our handle on it is, the greater the results. The chess analogy hits home because I know through empirical evidence that, if there is any hesitation on my part because I'm trying to find a note that fits the given harmony or I'm caught up in a fingering issue, the music will pay a price, especially when playing with a group. It messes with my entire flow. The best playing results come from being able to visualize all components of music on the fingerboard simultaneously. In order to be guided solely by the "inner music," it is imperative that we get well beyond thinking about the separate tools. Not doing so can often lead to careless mistakes and rigidity.

Our playing will benefit greatly if we have a game plan as elaborate as the ones possessed by leading figures in other fields. We need a holistic approach for revealing and removing obstacles—to eventually view the guitar neck as a world-class chess player views the chessboard; to have the focused balance between offense and defense of an elite boxer; to be able to transcend the negligible elements like the finest motocross riders do.

CONNECTION

It can never be emphasized enough: physical connection to one's instrument is a requisite to expressive playing. Technique is often thought of as the bridge to creating expressive playing. As true as that may be, technique is only part of the equation. While technique, as I see it, is a facet of growth that is continual and in flux in order to accommodate new data, it is used as a means to an end—to execute a continuation of musical goals. It is about execution.

Connectivity, however, might be seen as the underbelly of technique and can be cultivated distinctively in order to garner more cohesiveness between the body and guitar. Ultimately, one's technical prowess becomes stronger when focusing on the connective mechanics that are subtler. The better connected you are to the idiosyncratic nature of the guitar (e.g., right- and left-hand timing, dynamic range, attack sensitivity, tonal variation, sustain), the larger the potential to play more meaningful and spontaneous ideas that correlate with how you feel in the moment of execution—full improvisation.

In this and the following chapter, there are a few exercises that I've designed that will help strengthen this bond between expression, the body, and the guitar.

PHRASING

If you think about it, the way you choose to phrase a given set of notes should correlate with the way you feel, which ultimately guides what you play. For example, when you attack (pick) all the notes of a line, it projects a different feeling than if you attacked every other note, hammered onto some, and pulled off others. At the very least, picking a note creates a different impression and dynamic than hammering on or pulling off. This should be enough information to merit an investigation into phrasing variation.

Having the ability to phrase in a variety of ways not only helps a solo sound more interesting, but also aids us in connecting the guitar to a wider framework of feelings. On the contrary, if you always phrase in one way, which many players do, you may be forgoing the full opportunity of connecting mind/ear (ideas), heart (emotion), body (muscles), and guitar (interface).

Try the following exercise to see how you can expand on phrasing. What we are looking for here is to get to a point of "non-thinking" between the different phrases, and instead simply *hearing* the quality of phrases. Singing the phrase types will most definitely help us internalize and fully connect to the inner mechanics of each.

Once you have mastered these phrase types and can interchange them at ease, you should feel a sense of liberation in your playing.

For now, choose three consecutive notes on any one string (e.g., A–B–C). *Slowly* play through the following phrase-type combinations.

Ascending:
1. Pick all notes
2. Pick the first and second notes; hammer onto the third
3. Pick the first note; hammer onto the second; pick the third
4. Pick the first note; hammer onto the second and third
   (For more practice, try substituting slides in place of the hammer-ons.)

Descending:

1. Pick all notes
2. Pick the first and second notes; pull off to the third
3. Pick the first note; pull off to the second; pick the third
4. Pick the first note; pull off to the second and third

(For more practice, try substituting slides in place of the pull-offs.)

The most natural thing to do is to couple Ascending #1 with Descending #1, A2 with D2, and so on. You can also mix them up: A1/D3, etc. Eventually, you should be able to interchange phrasing with ease.

Below is a three-notes-per-string arrangement of the A Dorian mode. Ascending from the lowest A (string 6, fret 5) and using A2 and D2 (played as triplets), we would pick the notes A and B and then hammer onto the note C, following this pattern all the way through to the high E string. Descending, we would pick the notes D and C (string 1) and then pull off to the note B, following this pattern all the way back down to the low E string.

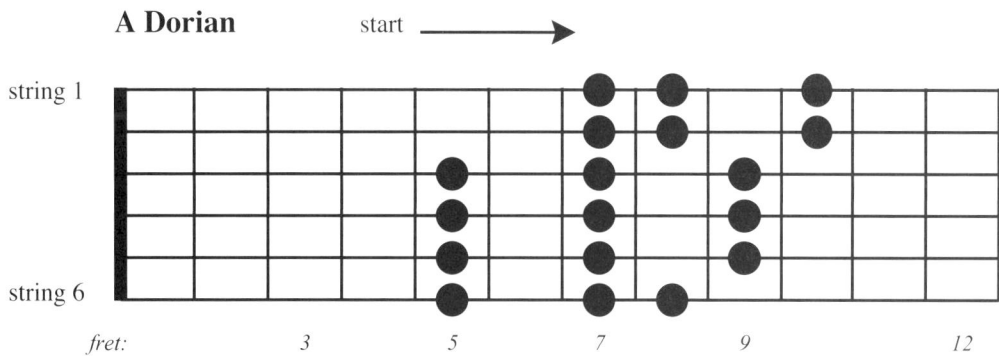

It becomes trickier to retain the phrasing when we play four eighth notes per two beats (as opposed to a triplet per one beat) while still using three notes per string. Here is the same example notated in triplets and eighth notes, played with the A2/D2 phrasing scheme:

Track 1 **A2/D2 triplets**

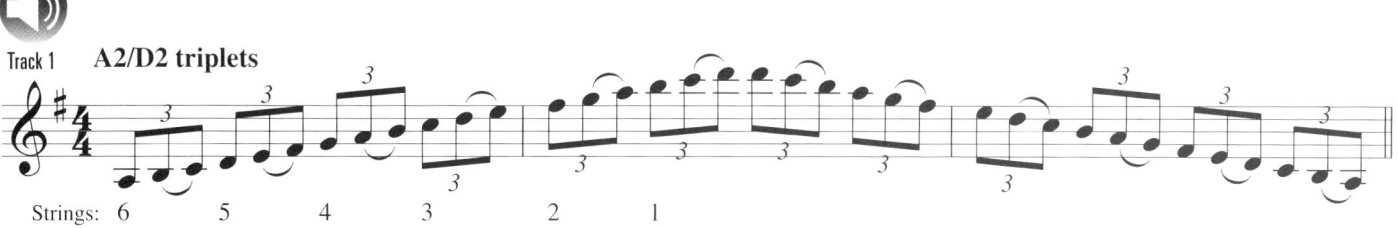

A2/D2 eighth notes

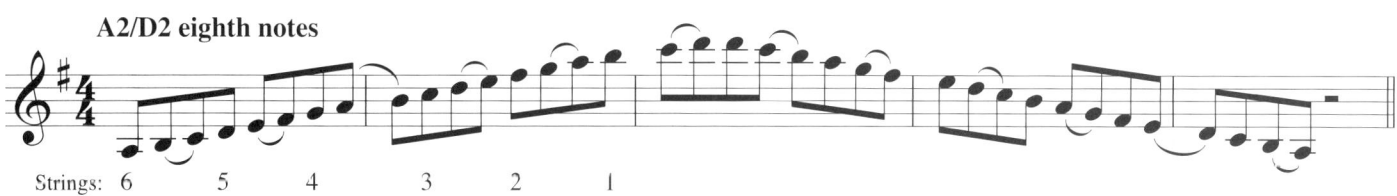

Now work all phrasing possibilities into your melodic ideas.

STACCATO PICKING

Ultimately, the goal of most players is to play effectively with the least amount of effort. When playing, the span of physical space between the pick and the string becomes a crucial factor in gauging and establishing effectiveness. Essentially, the left hand is what incites the notes, and the right hand is what elevates the sound of the notes; therefore, when the separation between the two is minimal, it lessens the effort and increases effectiveness.

Through studying classical guitar, I learned a right-hand fingerpicking exercise that made my attack more efficient. It mandated that whichever right-hand finger is used to sound a note must also be used to create a staccato effect for that same note. For instance, often when we play staccato notes, we lift our left hand off the note or we stop the sound with our right-hand palm. For this exercise, we wouldn't do any of that; instead, we rely only on the right-hand nail that plucks the string to also stop the note just after it is played. In this way, our right-hand muscles become accustomed to being cocked and ready for the next attack, and the amount of space between the plucking finger and string should eventually—and naturally—decrease. I transferred the exercise to a pick and found similar results.

This next exercise will help reduce the distance between your pick and the string, which will also help you achieve a stronger connection between both hands and a quicker response time when playing.

The diagrams below show four ways to approach each note. The longer arrows are the initial pick stroke (either up or down). The short arrows are what follow each pick stroke (these are used to achieve the staccato).

Track 2

Staccato Picking Pattern 1

Staccato Picking Pattern 2

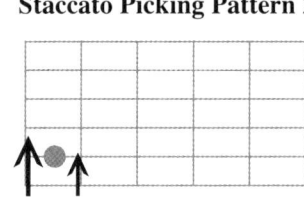

Staccato Picking Pattern 3

Staccato Picking Pattern 4

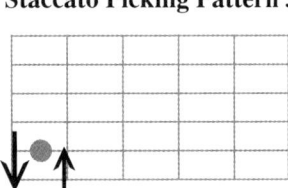
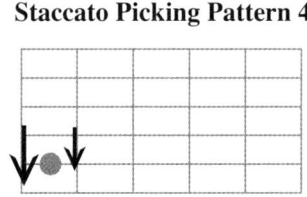

CONSECUTIVE SKIPPING

I constructed the following exercise so that my hands would work in tandem even while the notes are far apart. You'll notice that each note is played on a different string, which is essentially the driving factor behind this. I still use it to warm up, as I have for 25 years, because it helps me connect alternate (down/up) picking in order to create fluency. But, if you prefer different methods of picking other than alternate, it will still work for you.

We know it is rather easy to play fast scales. The goal of this exercise is to help you attain that same "scalar fortitude" even when the intervals between notes are significantly larger. As you practice, one goal might be to eventually get this to the same level of fluidity and precision that you maintain while playing fast scale passages.

The pattern is based on 5ths, with some exceptions. It starts out at the bottom of the neck in F and moves through the diatonic modes: F Ionian, G Dorian, A Phrygian, and so on.

Track 3   **Consecutive Skipping**

LONG TONES

Long tones are associated with saxophonists as a way to control breath, pitch, and note consistency. Try warming up by playing one note and hearing how long it can sustain. Of course, unlike in the movie *Spinal Tap*, you do need to play a note to hear the guitar sustain! This will help you become familiar with—and respect—the natural length of each note. It will also help you to connect with how *your* instrument breathes and speaks, as all guitars are not created equal. You can do it acoustically or while plugged into an amp.

EXPANDING EMOTIONAL AWARENESS

In Western music education, we are taught to play scales in all keys, in all directions, all fingerings, all octaves, etc. This is important, and though not all instrumentalists need to contend with directional variety or multiple fingerings, guitarists do. It is what most jazz guitarists practice for years to acquire a fluid sense of the fingerboard. However, there is a drawback to this type of exhaustive practice routine, one that easily distracts us from the musical and emotional potency that lies within the scales. Attention is given too often to the execution and memorization of scales as we "run" through the multitude of fingerings, but not to the "value" of each note within each scale. This section of the book makes an effort to reawaken our "musical awareness" of the raw materials—awareness that may have been overshadowed by practice itself.

A DIFFERENT MINDSET

Through my years of studying and performing with Indian classical musicians, I've been introduced to a very different approach to practicing the raw materials of music. Firstly, Indian musicians do not use scales to improvise, per se, but instead use very specific content within given pitch structures, or *ragas*—constructs that have been delineated into a codified system that is made up of emotionally charged directives. Improvising happens within these frameworks.

Any given raga is composed of several idiosyncratic nuances that include specific resolutions, phrases, ascending and descending distinctions, and gravitational pulls—all working in tandem to extract precise emotional and expressive content. Think of it like this: within one pitch structure (scale or mode), there can be several distinct ragas. For example, if we use the pitches from G Mixolydian to make up our own raga, we would add directives that would serve to codify a sound in order to evoke a specific feeling every time this raga is performed: skip the 6th when ascending, which would mean you can create melodies using the 6th *only* when descending; whenever playing the 3rd in descending fashion, approach it by sliding down from the 4th; often play a pattern that consists of the 2nd, 7th, and root, in that order. Now we have a specific sound, or character, with which to work and improvise from within the Mixolydian mode, and not simply the Mixolydian mode itself. To get a taste of how challenging this can be, try playing around with this constructed Mixolydian "raga" in order to bring out its unique essence. The first directive will stand throughout; the other two should be used at your discretion, all while improvising.

MELODY WITHOUT HARMONY

Indian classical music, whether it's Hindustani (North Indian) or Carnatic (South Indian), is most often played off of one tonic. I have performed entire concerts with Indian classical musicians using B♭ as the designated tonic, regardless of the raga that follows. Furthermore, often an entire concert will be dedicated to the unveiling of one raga. Imagine the placidity that needs to be in place for both the performer and the audience.

Most jazz musicians might justifiably think of playing in one tonality all night as a huge limitation, given that we're accustomed to shifting harmony and various tonal centers. In fact, because we're not trained to do so, it would most likely be cumbersome. I often wonder, by some miracle, how I would sound if I regained the time spent from the years of practicing harmony, voice leading, chromaticism, and 12 keys and replaced it with practicing the art of creating a "vibe" from melody, nuance, and rhythm—not dissimilar to what Indian classical artists are taught to do with the rendering of a raga. And to add to the miracle, if I retained all I do know about harmony, voice leading, and chromaticism. Coming back to reality, this awareness in thought at least brings attention to the nuance within some elements in my musical perception that may be weak.

Harmony is a great boon that most of us couldn't live without. However, as a jazz soloist, it can also musically work against us, albeit unconsciously, by camouflaging our task of creating a statement through melody. This is because harmony can instantly *fulfill* our need for color, change, and momentum; and subsequently, as long as we are playing over the progression, we are gratified. More so, since it can serve as a pattern inducer, and since the guitar is a visual instrument, we have a greater inclination to lean on "harmonic shift" as a crutch, therefore overlooking "melodic character." An effective paradigm or hierarchy (to avoid overshadowing melody) is to view harmony as subservient to melody, even though the harmony is dictating your melodic choices. In this way, when you're up against some staggering chord changes, you can be conscious about not getting caught up in playing on each chord, but rather creating a melodic thread using the changes.

Now, there are times when playing over each chord can sound great, but that's usually coupled with a concept. A good correlation to this is John Coltrane's superimposition of harmonic progressions. He designed a system that would allow him to yield more melodic variability over simple chord changes. When he recorded his tune "Giant Steps," his approach to soloing on it was very direct, as that was what the concept merited. We can see as his experimentation continued through the years, how he was less inclined to play directly over harmony and more in favor of stretching out melodic content. I, for one, would love to have heard how he would've played that tune in his later years. Nevertheless, once those harmonic doors were opened to the world, my feeling is that there was an even greater respect warranted towards the onus of creating a substantial melodic statement within a color-filled canvas.

Overall, a good thing to remember is what we actually have: sound, notes, music, and history. The *sound* we create comes from our instrument, fingers, imagination, etc.; the *notes* we have are the same for everyone; the *music* (or expression) is essentially what reflects our uniqueness and hinges on reaching beyond the raw materials. *History* allows us to evaluate the evolution of music and use that information to guide us in our creative endeavors, adding (however moderately) to the canon.

A striking Western parallel to Indian classical music can be made with the blues. B.B. King and other legendary blues players do not rely on harmony, per se, and thus place greater emphasis on creating a vibe through more universal means: timbre, melodic development, discerning note choice, various phrasing, dynamics, etc.—all within the parameters of a blues scale.

Just as in Indian classical music, blues can easily be weakened and spoiled by over-emphasizing the "emptiness" of raw materials such as scales, arpeggios, technique, or constantly varying the emotional vibe. Although jazz is a different kind of music, improvisation is a common thread between all three genres and so the question must be asked: why shouldn't the aforementioned apply to jazz players, as well? Or, to state it in a different way, does all the freedom that comes with harmony and chromaticism exclude the musical responsibility of creating a vibe while improvising?

This section puts into action some ways Indian classical methodology has impacted me to think more musically.

EMOTION-TO-SCALE RATIO

Applying the full umbrella of raga-based playing might not work so easily for what we do as jazz musicians. We can, however, grasp the idea of creating more from what we already have—that is, taking more advantage of *how* we approach notes and modes in general. Here is a simple exercise I have used with many students that helps to facilitate a better musical awareness. If you can record yourself doing the following, you will find it valuable at the end. If you do not record it now, it will not be as revealing.

- Play the A Dorian mode from the bottom A (sixth string) to the top A (first string) straight through without skipping notes.
- Take a moment to listen back and be as objective as you can when listening. Ask yourself: "Is this the most emotion I can pull from a scale?" and "Did I take this scale for granted since I viewed it as a scale and not music?" If the answer is "no" and "yes," respectfully, as it has

been for every student I've done this with, then you are being objective and have an opportunity in front of you to grow.

- Next, play the same scale again but with a magnified sense of feeling, like a solo. Listen back and ask/answer the same questions before proceeding.

GIVING VOICE TO THE INSTRUMENT

Finally, the larger point: now that you know how you sound when playing a good old scale in a manner that comes naturally, let's see what you are missing. In playing the scale, did you use any of the following?

- Staccato
- Bending
- Hammer-ons
- Pull-offs
- Short or long notes
- Slides—forward or back
- Harmonics
- Open strings/notes
- Dynamics
- Accents
- Vibrato

If you did use any combination of three or more, you are ahead of the game. But not to worry if you did not; like most of us, we have been trained to run up and down scales without giving them much thought. We just assume "a scale is a scale," and it is something we practice by default. Try it again while applying all of the previous directives.

This exercise may have seemed like a trick but, in fact, it shows us just how narrow our approach to playing can be. Now that you are more aware, you will keep the options at your fingertips when soloing or rendering a melody.

The variety of approaches to playing expressively is always there for us, but if we are clouded by unawareness, we may not see the sun.

NINE EMOTIONS (Navarasa)

Another revealing exercise, one that I have recently discovered by way of performing with South Indian dancers and musicians, works with specific emotions. *Navarasa* is an exploration of emotions manifested through the performing arts via facial expressions. *Nava* means "nine," and *rasa* means "emotion" or "juice."

In a recent Carnatic dance performance I was involved with, the band was asked to create musical improvisations based on nine distinct emotions depicted by the dancers. Each emotion carried a specific raga and would correlate with the dancers.

The initial attempt (in rehearsal) made me cognizant of how limited my playing had become, both dynamically and emotionally. Being forced and put on the spot to convey a feeling, even if I did not feel it, was a challenge I welcomed. I found the exercise jarring at first but realized it was not dissimilar to the role-playing that actors must go through. But I am not an actor, and jazz musicians do not work off of prescribed feelings when they solo, so what could I learn from this? Acting imposes a level of specificity that jazz does not; however, I soon realized that, while playing jazz seems to be the inverse of acting, in some ways it operates in a similar manner. In other words, whatever we *do* play ideally should be a reflection of what we *are* feeling, whether that feeling is manufactured (actor) or spontaneous (musician).

Moving through the process of *Navarasa* also reaffirmed the notion that when we are improvising on original music or jazz standards, we actually are working off of prescribed feelings, better known as the *tune*. If a tune doesn't contain a built-in quality, mood, or feeling, then it's likely a weak tune. Essentially, we are extending a vibe. Of course, if we are playing totally free form, this obviously applies much less because of having no prescribed vibe to work from. Given these factors, I found it interesting in this setting to be given only a scale and one emotion at a time to build from.

expanding emotional awareness

Following is a list of nine emotions, along with randomly prescribed scales, all using C as the tonic. The objective of this exercise is to stretch your canvas of feelings *on the guitar* by honing in on each. For now, you should exaggerate, particularly when the emotions are disparate (e.g., Love should sound very different from Anger). It becomes more difficult when you have two emotions that are similar, such as Love/Peace or Anger/Fear. That is why exaggerating makes each feeling more musically apparent and ultimately widens our spectrum of applied emotions.

With this exercise, the notes do not need to move through the scale in sequential order—so just play! (Record this, as well.)

Nine Emotions

A different (and much more challenging) way to approach this would be to use one mode for all of the emotions. This will narrow the raw materials considerably and force us not to depend on the inherent change of feeling within the scale. Choose C Ionian (a very transparent scale) and run through all nine emotions.

I'm certain that, once you have worked through this section of the book, your emotions will be more directly connected to the guitar.

GAINING CONTROL

Having control over musical components via the guitar is necessary in order to fully express oneself.

By "control," I do not mean playing ideas in the same predetermined and limited manner or playing the same licks—unless, of course, that is what you are going for. What I'm referring to is akin to the seemingly limitless musical control that the greatest jazz players possess. Their playing has a consistency that can only come from having command over their instrument, their mind, and ultimately their music. That strength and consistency, combined with imagination and creativity, empowers humans to express fully and freely without sounding over-practiced.

Separating the components allows us to customize exercises within each in order to gain control over them. Below are a few that will get you started.

THE FIVE COMPONENTS

1. MELODY

Extending Vocabulary (by force)

To test our melodic resource, a helpful thing to do is play over a standard like "Stella by Starlight" but double the length of the chords. The chords, as they are, last four beats each: four beats of Em7♭5, four beats of A7, and so forth. When we solo over this, each chord color passes quickly, even at ballad tempo. What often ends up happening, perhaps subconsciously, is that we find comfort zones on the neck that guide us through each quick change of harmony, not forcing ourselves to look elsewhere. In other words, we can get away with making a statement in the same *habitual* area and quickly move to the next chord.

Making the changes twice as long forces us to come up with longer statements over each chord, which essentially means two things: 1) we are more likely to develop other parts of the neck that may have been overlooked within four beats, and 2) we have to be more creative in order to sustain interest during the extended time. The harmonic changes now can be thought of as a succession of micro modal shifts.

Harmony can easily become a diversion from playing something that is meaningful. As long as we are playing over the changes, we can feel gratified and not know we are falling into *limiting* traps. This exercise shines a light on possible weaknesses.

Furthermore, since many of the chords in standards are generally related to one another, it takes even greater effort to find and emphasize *non-common tones* versus *common tones*. Since the chords last longer, it becomes crucial to create inner harmonic/melodic movement via voice leading.

I've constructed a line on the next page that runs through the first passage of "Stella," lengthened. Be cognizant of voice leading, common tones, and non-common tones, as well as your neck positions. The circled notes are what differentiate the chord-scales and create the inner movement from chord to chord.

gaining control

Track 4 "Stella by Starlight" extending vocabulary

Target Specificity

Another important step in gaining control of melody with your instrument is being able to target any harmonic tone on any beat. After all, resolution and where and how you place it is a big part of how your music will sound.

Start practicing targeting in a simple way. Let's decide we are going to place emphasis on the 7th of every chord and place that on the fourth beat of every bar. This may come off sounding stiff but it will strengthen our targeting abilities. Here is an example on "Stella":

Track 5 "Stella by Starlight" target specificity

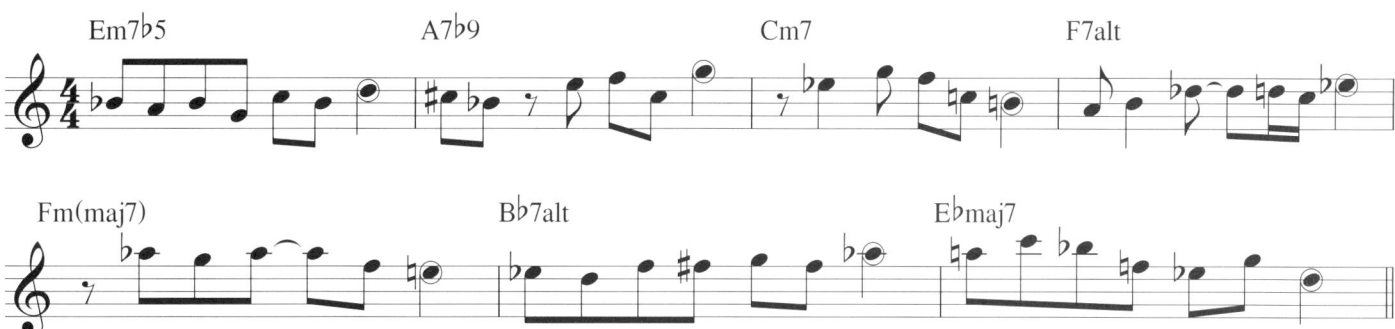

Adding other elements to targeting creates further interest.

Suspension

Now we will suspend our resolutions by playing the 7th of each chord on the upbeat of beat 4 and tying the note into the following bar. This creates a nice effect because the notes are not always directly common to each chord and therefore a bit of tension is imposed over the bar line.

Track 6 "Stella by Starlight" targeting specificity by suspension

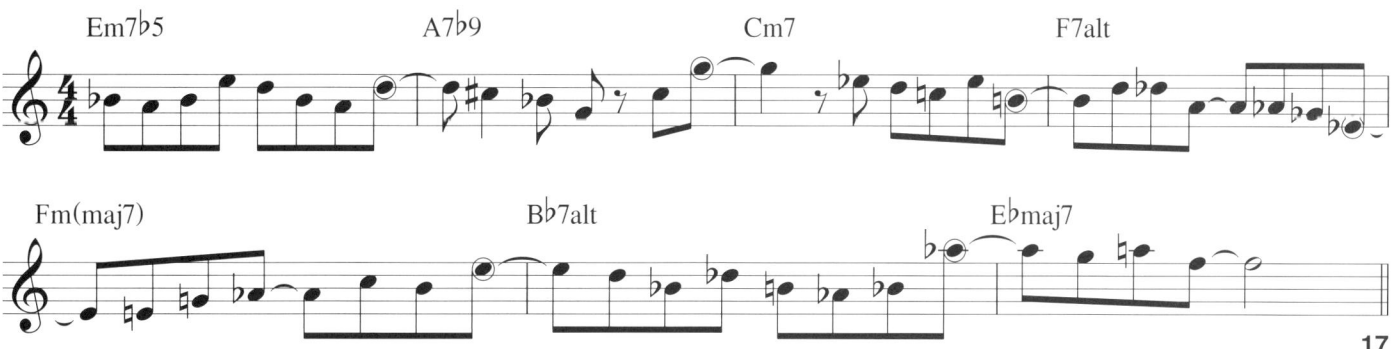

Anticipation

A different way to approach the inner phrasing is by anticipating what is coming up. Play the 7th of the following chord on the upbeat of beat 4 of the preceding measure. We are literally jumping ahead an eighth note.

Track 7 "Stella by Starlight" targeting specificity by anticipation

You can sense the underlying discipline that is needed when there are parameters placed on soloing. Take it a step further and choose triplets or 16th notes for your targeted notes.

2. HARMONY

Chord Fragments (Intervallic Combinations of Three Notes Per Chord)

Using "Stella" as our framework, we will again treat each mode from each chord as micro modal shifts. This will allow us to slowly work the neck as we build chord voicings made up of predetermined interval combinations.

The first chord is Em7♭5. We can consider it either a Locrian (the seventh chord of F major) or Locrian with a ♮2nd (the sixth chord of G melodic minor). Let's go with the latter since the F♯ from the major 2nd is more in line with the historically accurate initial chord of B♭°(maj7). (This is a good time to interject that the harmony I'm using in my samples are "jazz" changes that I've learned over the years, not always the original. It's good to research how standards have evolved harmonically.) Initially, we'll randomly choose an interval combination; for example, a 2nd, 6th, and 4th (through experience, I know this one works well). Then we will build a voicing from the given intervals. Starting from the root, E, will render the following: the interval of a 2nd from E is F♯; from F♯, go up a 6th to D; and from D, go up a 4th to G. Take note that the interval type (major, minor, or perfect) is predetermined by the diatonic mode. For instance, we selected a 6th for our second interval. From F♯, the 6th will have to be a *minor* 6th, or D♮, because there is no D♯ (major 6th) in the E Locrian mode.

So, the notes of the 2nd/6th/4th intervallic set are: F♯, D, and G.

The next step would be to move that interval shape horizontally all the way up and down the fretboard. For now, we'll do this on strings 6, 4, and 3. You may notice that the intervals will need to shift a little as you move through the neck in order to stay within the chosen Locrian ♮2nd mode. For example, 6ths might go from minor to major as we move up, 4ths from perfect to augmented (i.e., tritone), etc.

gaining control

For each of the following examples, use these different playing approaches:

1. Play black set (F♯/D/G), gray set (G/E/A), and continue up the neck

2. Play only black, then only gray up the neck

3. Arpeggiate all

4. Mix all notes together randomly

Track 8

String set 6/4/3

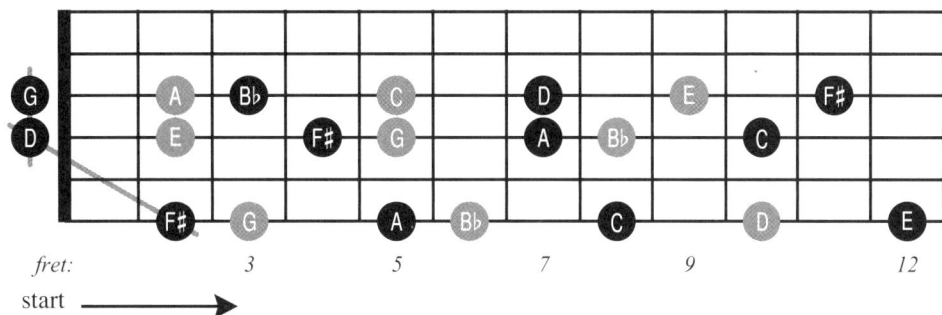

Try the same for string sets 5/3/2 and 4/2/1. Start at the indicated spot and continue to the end of the fretboard. Then return to the starting point and continue in the opposite direction to the other end of the fretboard.

Track 9

String set 5/3/2

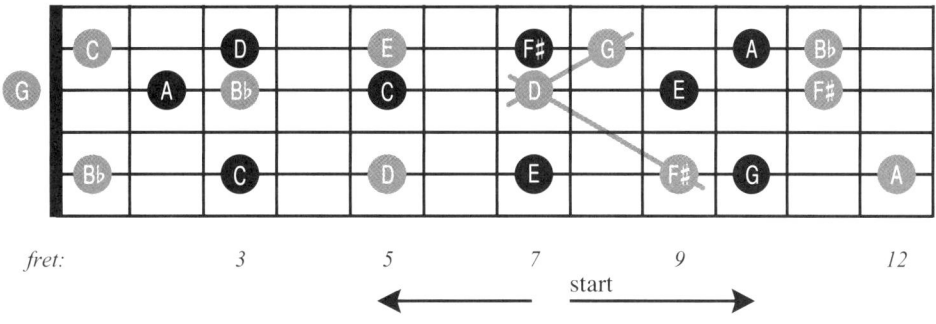

Track 10

String set 4/2/1

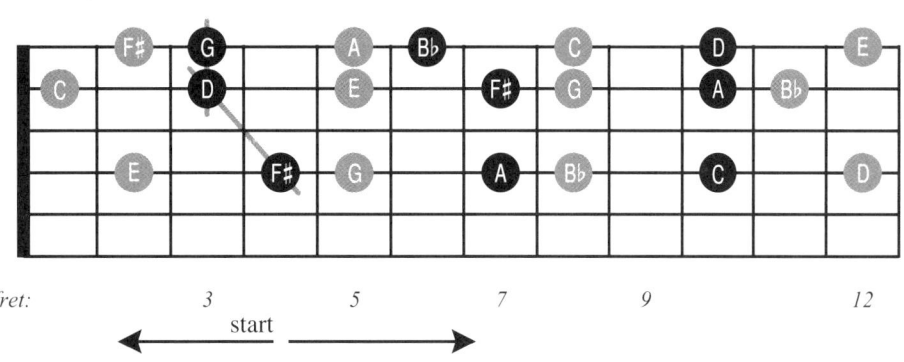

19

Now try the same in vertical fashion (while still in E Locrian ♮2nd) and then move it up the neck:

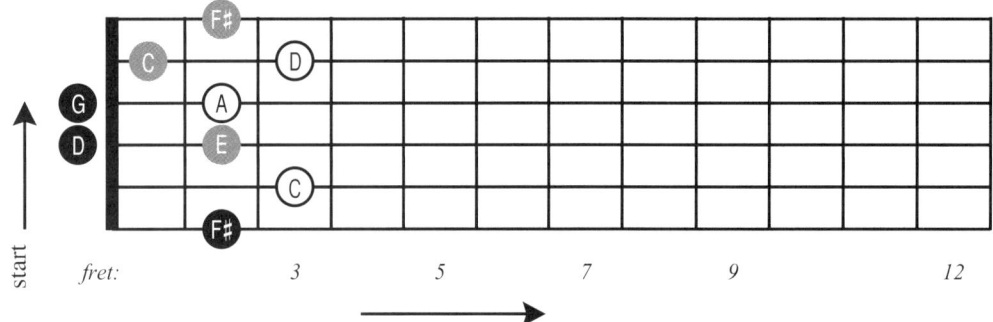

Track 11

Now work the A altered scale (B♭ melodic minor) up the neck:

A altered scale

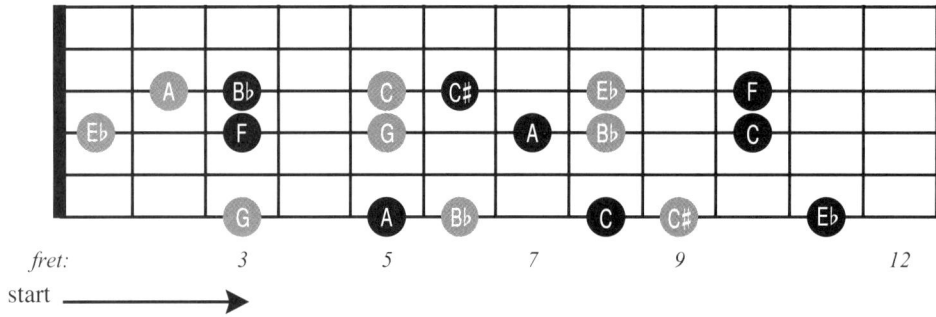

By the time you work this shape through an entire tune, you should be very well acquainted with the fretboard.

The following is an expanded version of how I would apply intervallic structures to "Stella." I started with our 2nd/6th/4th structure and began weaving through the harmony, purely directed by simple voice leading. Below each chord, you will see the interval/numeric content.

What you can gather from this is that there are many shapes that can be put into use within one passage. You can choose whichever ones speak to you and move them through full tunes.

Track 12

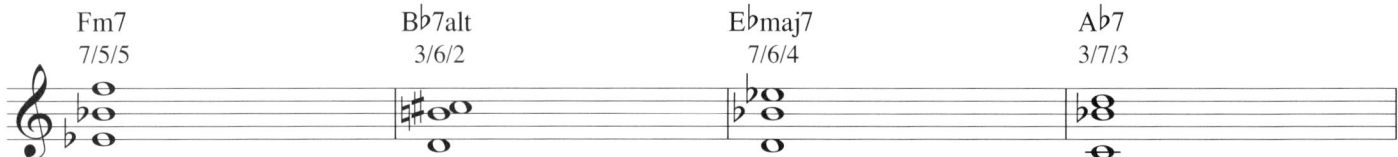

Voice Leading

The following exercise is indispensable. I learned it from my great teacher Paul La Rose many years ago and continue to expand, use, and teach it. At first, it will seem like a melodic exercise, but I chose to place it in the harmony category because it is really about voice leading through harmony.

Choose a mode—say, Lydian—and start on the low F since it's the bottom of the guitar. Next, play any Fmaj7#11 voicing and create a progression by moving it up in major 2nds. This will give us a Lydian progression, starting on these roots: F, G, A, B, D♭, and E♭. After the progression is established in your head, play four consecutive scale (F Lydian) notes—F, G, A, and B—starting from the first chord, Fmaj7#11. Next, play four scale notes from G Lydian (G–A–B–C#–D–E–F#)

but continue from where you left off; in this case, after the note B. So, the second phrase would start on C♯ and continue on with three more G Lydian notes: D, E, and F♯. We would do the same in A Lydian (A–B–C♯–D♯–E–F♯–G♯), which will give us G♯, A, B, and C♯. This continues up the neck and back down until you establish a flow without any pauses. You can do it with a metronome, playing each pitch as a quarter, eighth, or 16th note. Also, you can record the progression first in order to hear the voice leading while playing over it.

Track 13

Voice Leading

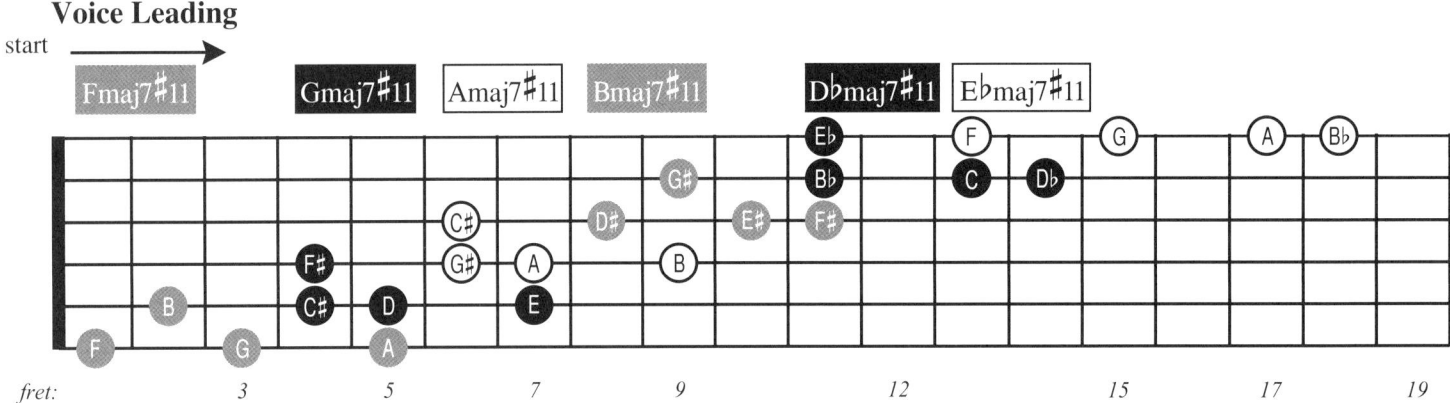

When you feel comfortable with this progression, do the same but with a different space between the chords; for example, half steps (F, F♯, G, G♯, etc.) or minor 3rds (F, A♭, B, D, etc.). Furthermore, you can also change the quality of the mode with each chord movement. As an example, if we were to keep the distance a whole step between chords, the first mode could remain F Lydian, the second could be G Phrygian, the third A Mixolydian, and so on. You can go even further and use a mixture of diatonic and "exotic" modes (e.g., harmonic major) in the same progression.

This entire process can also be plugged into a standard that you may be struggling with—perhaps "Stella by Starlight." It is important to remember that this is a scale/fingerboard exercise and therefore you should not be concerned with outlining the chords with the "best" notes; instead, simply get your *navigation skills* stronger by staying inside the proper scales.

Track 14

"Stella by Starlight"

Em9♭5: E Locrian ♮2, from G melodic minor
A7♯5: A Super Locrian, from B♭ melodic minor
Cm7: C Dorian
F7: F Mixolydian ♯4, from C melodic minor
Fm7: F melodic minor
B♭13♭9: B♭ half/whole diminished

gaining control

Track 15

Let's try moving the scales in a different direction. Below, I am starting from the 3rd of F major (A) in order to use more of the fretboard.

Starting on A, string 6

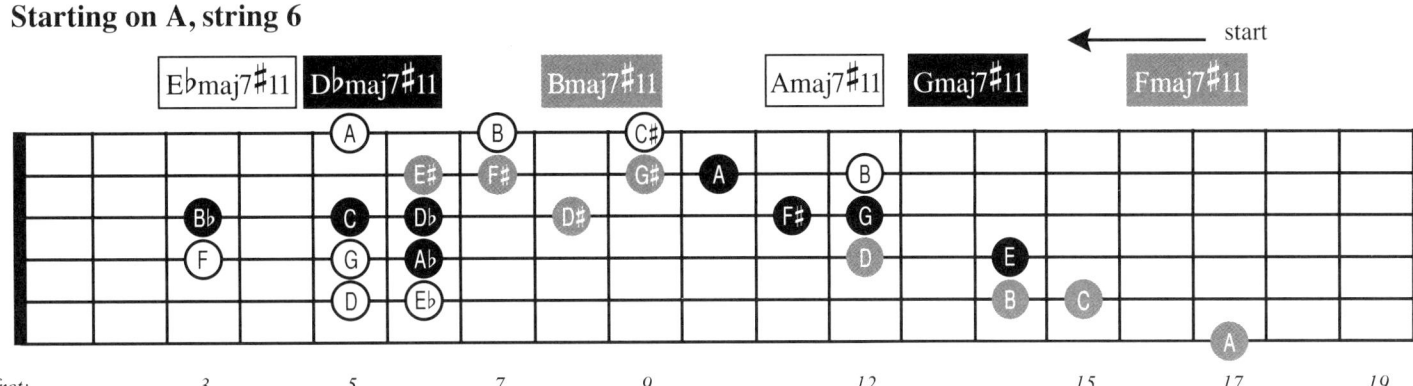

Track 16

And now starting from the first string…

Starting on F, string 1

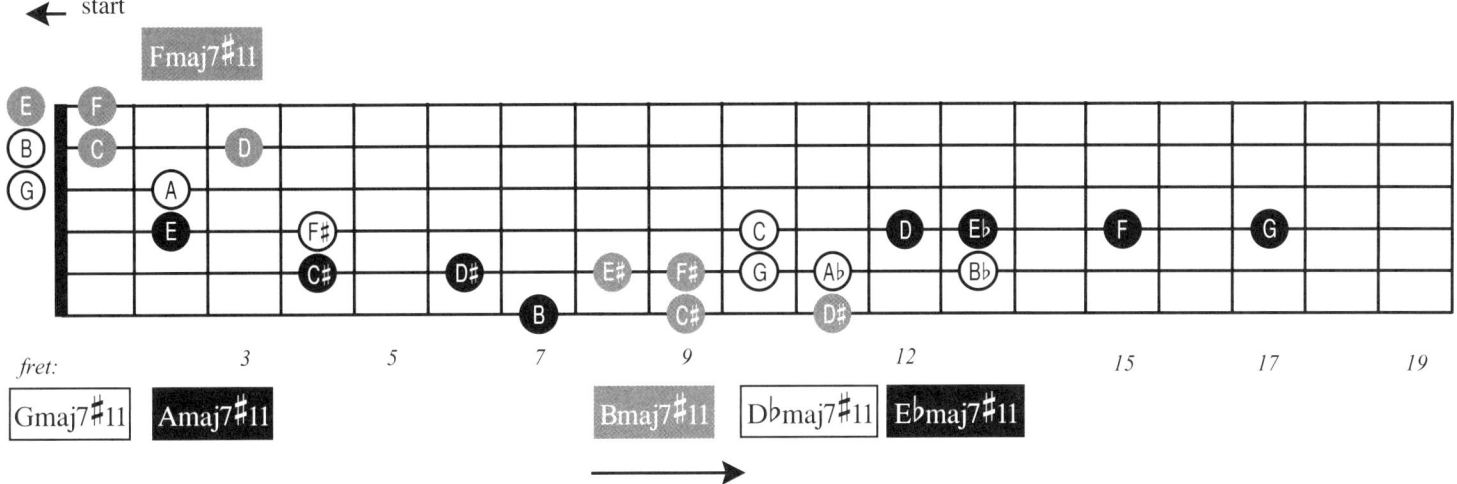

Using Chord Tones

Track 17

We will now outline the chords by implementing the same exercise but with arpeggios—using mostly 3rds rather than half or whole steps.

Starting on F, string 6

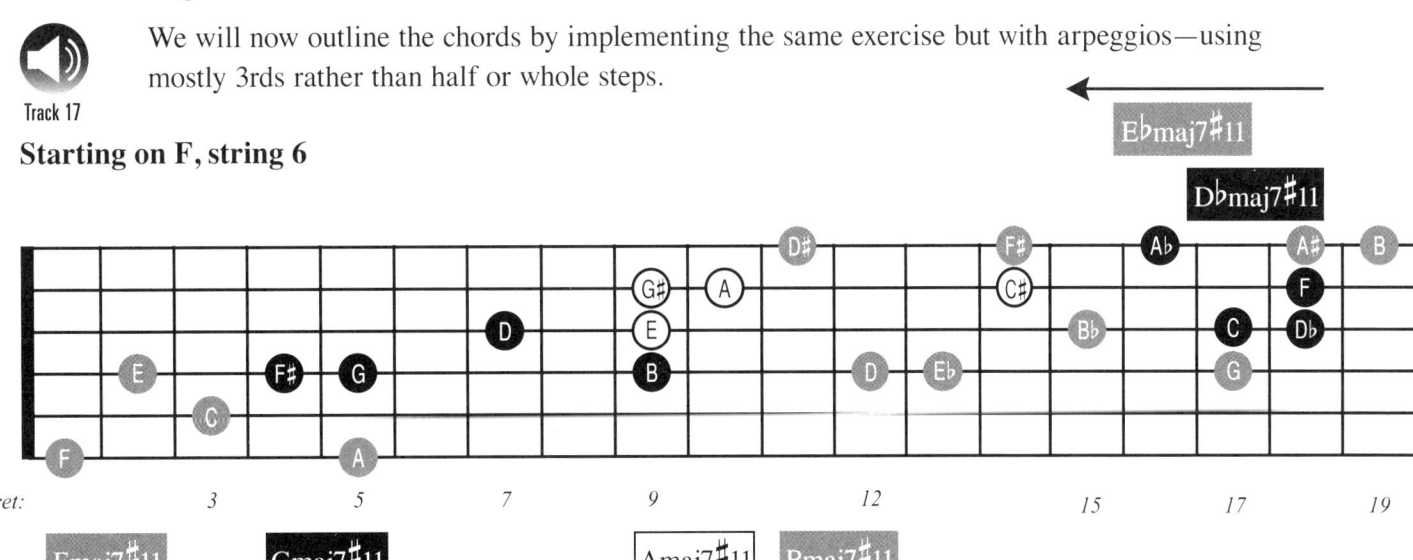

3. RHYTHM
Starting Phrases from Various Places

It is always important to know where the downbeat is, but that awareness often tricks us into starting phrases on downbeats. The following exercise is designed to help us feel various points from which we can start our phrases. It may seem cumbersome, but after you have gone through it with a metronome, you should notice a change in the way you position your phrases. Here, we are in 4/4, but applying this to different meters will generate different feelings.

gaining control

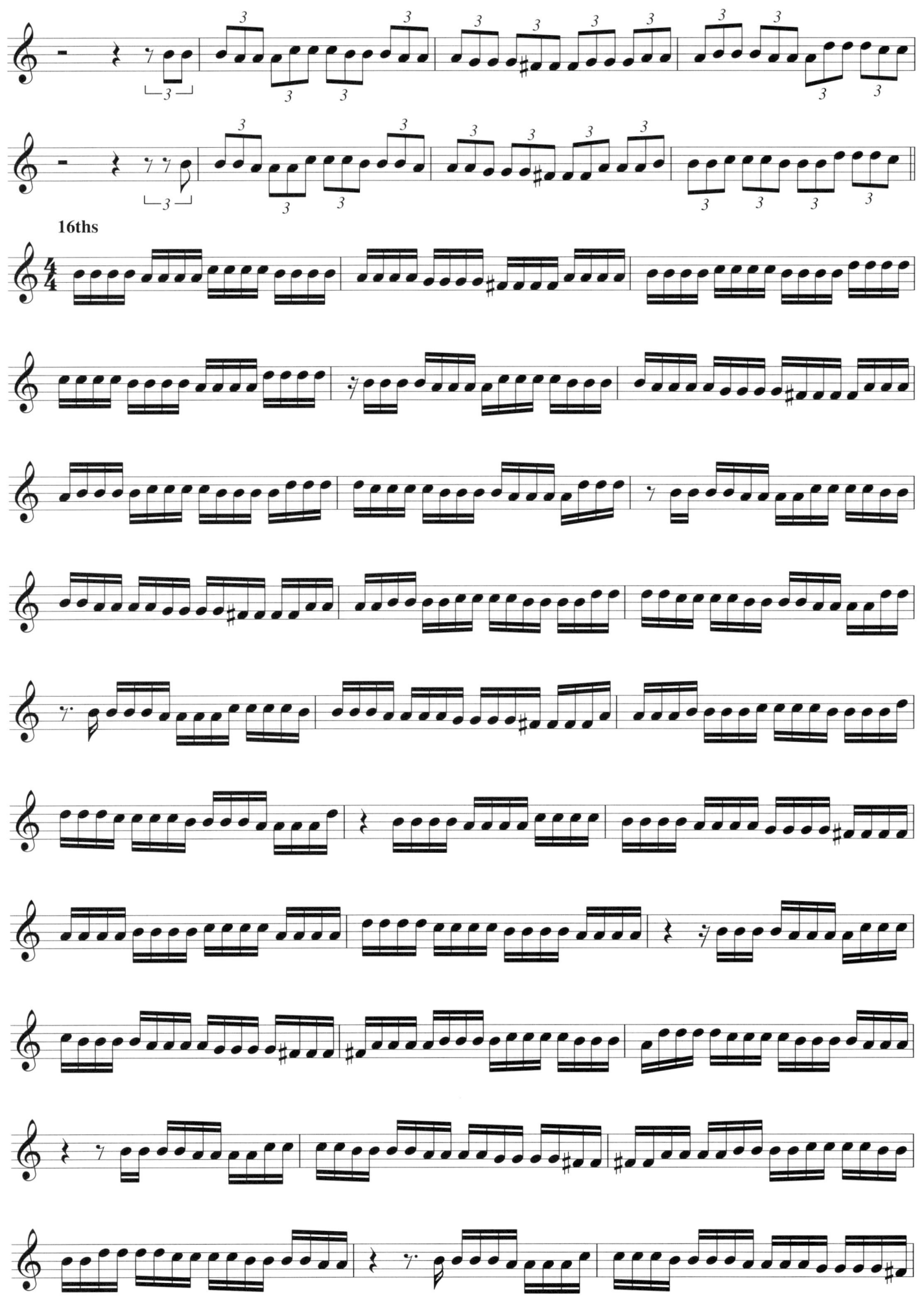

gaining control

Playing in Various Meters

Playing music in so-called "odd" meters can be challenging. Even if we decide to only play in 4/4 the rest of our lives, practicing in odd meters can force us out of our comfort zone. Five-beat cycles have made me uncomfortable, so I've chosen to work with that meter; however, you can apply the following exercise to any meter. It will help you feel accents in unusual places.

Here, the exercise uses just one note. The accompanying audio track goes through the full exercise once, and then leaves several minutes of empty clicks for you to practice the exercise over yourself:

Track 18 **Quarters**

Eighths

Eighths in quintuplets (accented in fives)

Triplets

Triplets in quintuplets

16ths

16ths in quintuplets

Quintuplets

gaining control

And now with a scale:

Track 19 **A minor**

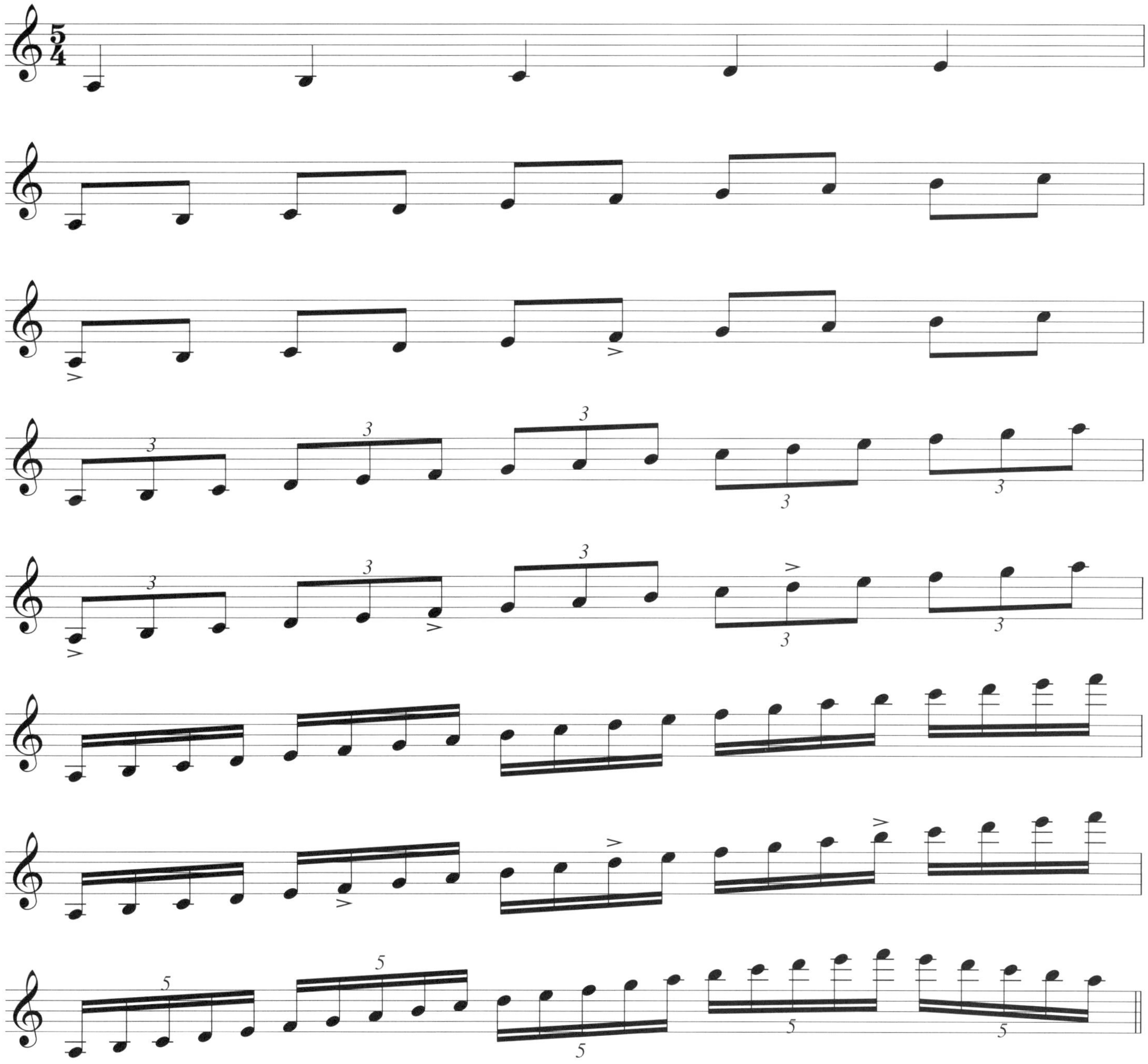

Implying 7/8 over 4/4

The following chart shows how to imply 7/8 over 4/4 in an eight-bar phrase. Whether or not you use it in a real situation is not the point, but mastering the feel will serve as a springboard for embracing more syncopation.

If we play 7/8 eight times, the downbeat of the eighth 7/8 phrase will meet on the downbeat of the eighth 4/4 bar. So, we are left with an extra bar of four quarters (the eighth bar). If, for this eighth bar, we continue to think in 7/8, we would be left with one extra eighth note after adding that ninth 7/8 phrase. A different way to approach it is to play 7/8 eight times and treat the eighth bar as one bar of 4/4. The latter may feel easier.

So, the scheme will either be: 7/8 x **9** + 1 eighth note, or 7/8 x **8** + 1 bar of 4/4.

Track 20 **7/8 over 4/4**

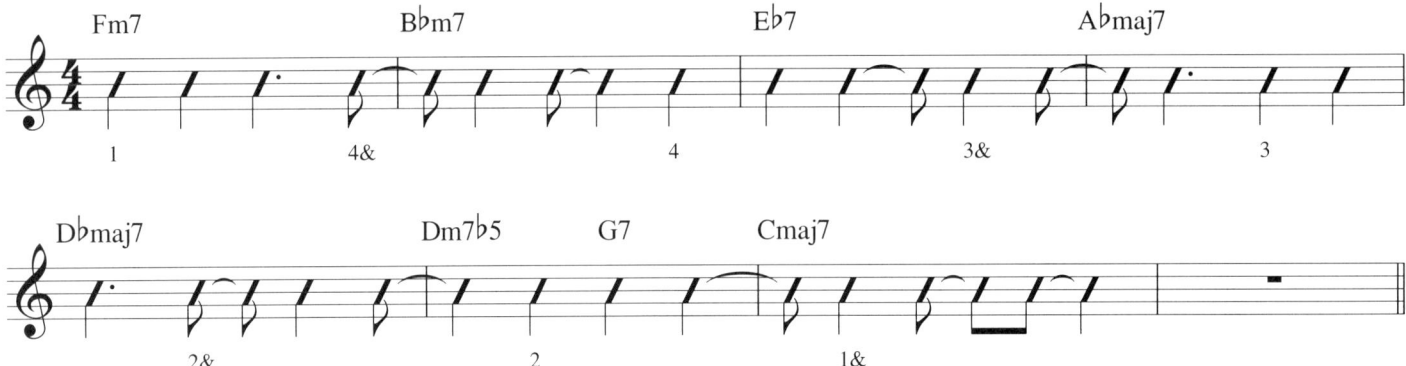

- The numbers correspond to accents of 7/8 within 4/4 meter and the beat the accents start from.
- Memorize the scheme of beats to play 7/8 within 4/4. For example, 1; 4&; 4; 3&; 3, etc.
- Start lines from these designated accents.

Implying 4/4 over 7/8

Play around with the following, as well.

Track 21 **4/4 over 7/8**

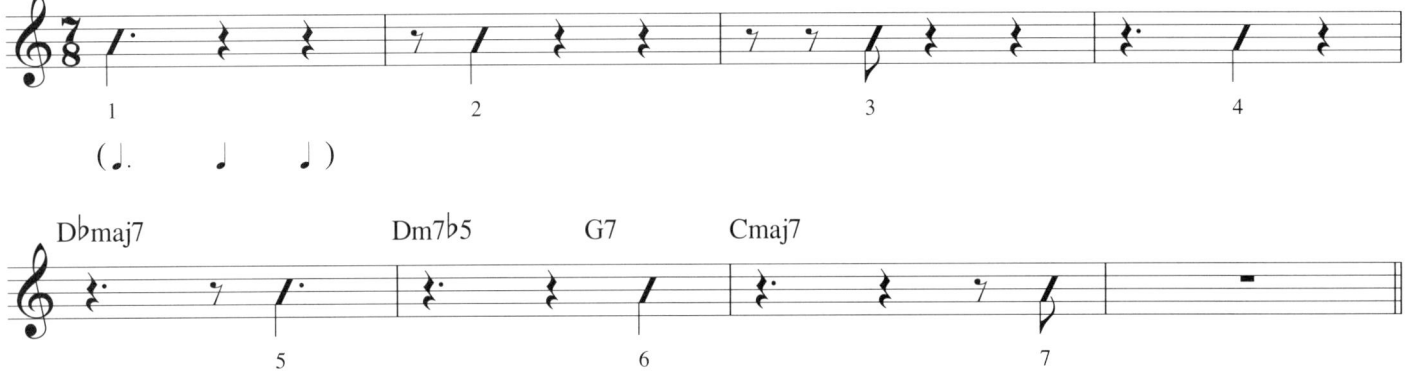

- The numbers correspond to accents of 4/4 within 7/8 meter and the beat (8th note) the accents start from.
- It takes 7 bars of 4/4 to complete the phrase.
- Memorize the scheme of beats to play 4/4 within 7/8.

Implying 7/8 over 7/4

Track 22 7/8 over 7/4

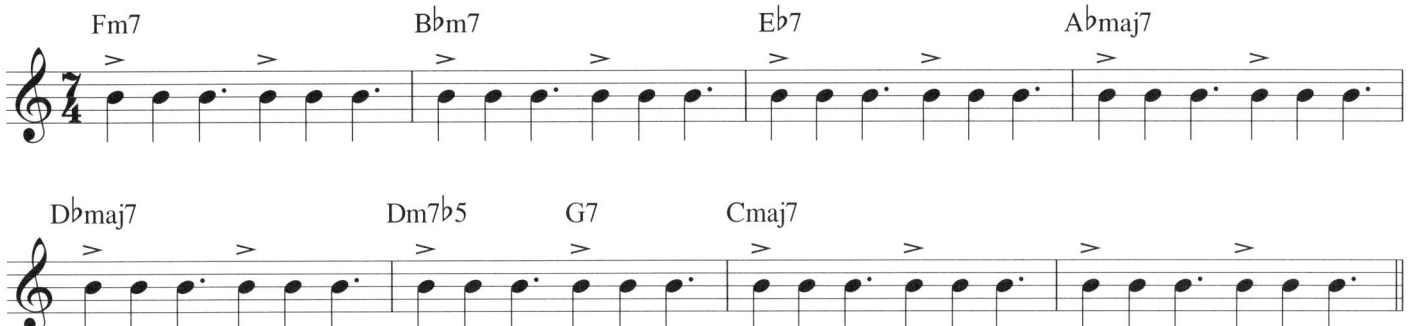

- This is more straightforward, as everything lines up on the downbeats.
- Accent the downbeats of each phrase of 7/8.

South Indian Rhythm Exercise

Carnatic (South Indian classical) is a highly complex music that contains many facets. One facet that translates well to jazz is its mathematical rhythmic nature. This aspect alone can be studied throughout life and one may still only scratch the surface. But, as a searching and growing jazz musician, I found it very useful to get even a rudimentary sense of what it feels like to be involved in the nature of these rhythms.

Below is a simple Carnatic exercise that is designed to strengthen our sense of displacement. Again, most Carnatic rhythms contain displacement, and so by mastering the following, you may get a sense of what the feeling of Carnatic rhythm can convey.

The pattern here is based on groupings of 16th notes played with four or five notes per accented phrase. We phrase and accent as such: 4 4 4 5 / 4 4 4 5 / 4 4 4 5 / 4 4 5. This will lead us back to the downbeat in a 16-beat cycle (or four bars of 4/4) and we can start the cycle over.

Try the following by vocalizing the numbers that correspond to the 16th notes while clapping the quarter notes along with a metronome. (Always accent the downbeat of every 4/4 measure with the clap.)

Track 23

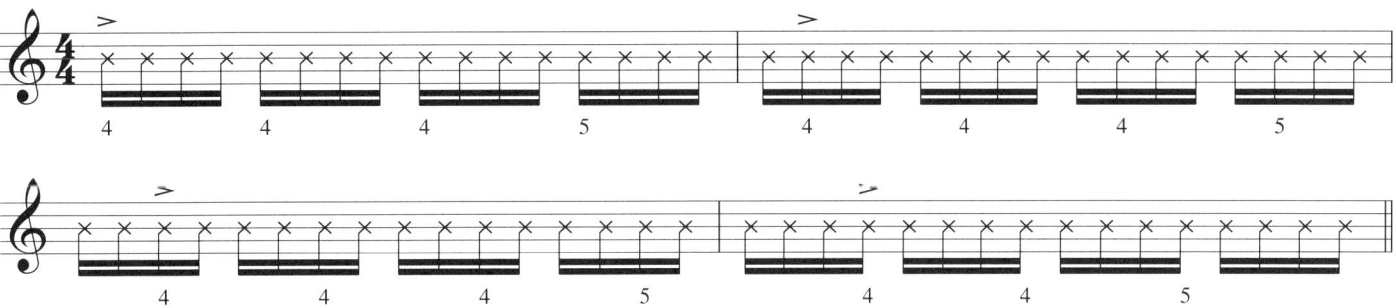

Here it is with notes added:

Track 24

Ride Pattern

In my estimation (and probably many others), the forward momentum, feel, and sound of jazz are best conveyed through the drums and, more specifically, the ride cymbal. If you haven't played a ride cymbal, you may want to in order to get the feel of the bounce that drummers are connected to.

Another route is to use the guitar as a ride cymbal. Physically, it is very different, but the goal is to simply elicit the bounce of a stick to cymbal. Bringing our attention to what is viewed as the crux of the jazz feel benefits us greatly. The ride pattern of great drummers helps us hear how to feel and break up the beat—something well worth imitating.

Playing out of the Pocket

My wife is a professional Hindustani Indian vocalist and she once (or 10 times) pointed out to me how most jazz instrumentalists, myself included, play directly on the beat. Looking back on my own education and practice, my attention was mostly placed on instrumentalists (not vocalists), due in no small part to the multifaceted content they display within extended soloing. This is why I think it is beneficial for me to consciously practice playing out of the pocket (i.e., less on top of the beat) while feeling the pocket, much like a vocalist.

You might want to try this yourself: first, play solid eighth notes as you usually would and with a metronome. Then do the same, but this time, vary the lengths of some notes by minimal time—kind of like a push-pull effect within the beat. This kind of playing is a little different than playing over the bar line, which is more direct. It is more akin to playing around the bar line and allowing the melody to breathe. If you need a reference, listen to Billie Holiday or perhaps the great Indian classical vocalists Bhimsen Joshi and Kishori Amonkar, while clapping the beats.

Three Placements

Another way to test our sense of time within a pulse is to play an entire phrase in three ways:

1. Behind (laidback)
2. Center (straight)
3. Ahead (on top)

Most of us will play in all three ways at some point; however, it may be good to practice in all ways just in case you tend to play the same 98 percent of the time. I would advise recording these variations, as well.

gaining control

4. TECHNIQUE (muscle development)

Right-Hand Technique Exercises

Bhangra

Bhangra is folk music from the state of Punjab; it is an Indian music genre that is based on a hard-driving groove. Below is a fragment in this style that I use as an exercise to build muscles and connect both hands. At first, the right hand may need more attention, but eventually the challenge is to get it to flow in tempo with both hands working in tandem—similar to a good Bhangra dancer who is fully connected to their entire body. Try it in various tempos.

Track 25 **Bhangra**

Try different picking:

- all up
- all down
- down-up
- up-down

Alternate Picking in Threes

Alternate picking means down-up or up-down, thus it's made up of two movements. If we apply this picking to combinations of three notes, it becomes odd within the even pick strokes, and therefore more challenging. Below is a good, challenging exercise made up of three-note phrases in intervals of 4ths, along with several ways to approach (i.e., pick) this exercise that will surely make for a tricky muscle/mind connection feat.

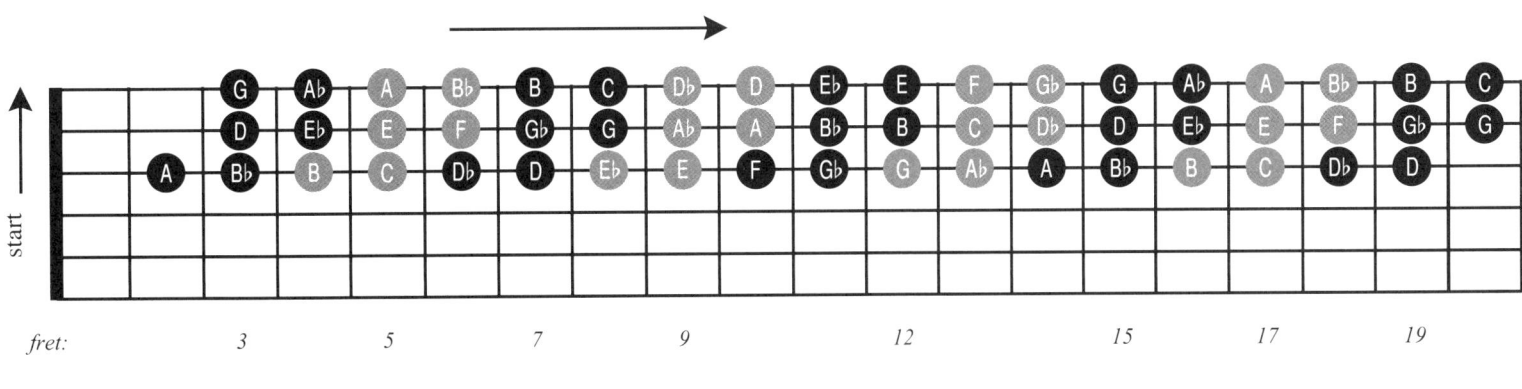

Strings	3/2/1	1/2/3	3/2/1	1/2/3	1/2/3	1/2/3	3/2/1	3/2/1	2/1/3	2/1/3	3/2/1	2/3/1	1/2/3	2/1/3	2/3/1	3/2/1	1/3/2	3/2/1
Picking	d/u/d*	u/d/u	u/d/u	d/u/d	d/u/d	u/d/u	u/d/u	d/u/d	u/d/u	d/u/d	u/d/u	d/u/d	u/d/u	d/u/d	u/d/u	d/u/d	u/d/u	d/u/d

*d = downstroke   u = upstroke

- Repeat these in pairs in order to create an alternative picking exercise.
- Try them straight through to work alternative and non-alternative picking.

Left-Hand Technique Exercises

Play a solo with combinations of two fingers:

1–2   2–3   3–4   1–3   1–4   2–4

(1 = index, 2 = middle, 3 = ring, 4 = pinky)

Playing in this manner helps us gain independence in the left hand. It pushes distinct muscles, unlike continuously playing with all fingers.

Play a solo using only your left hand (no picking)

I like doing this on occasion to see if I can pull it off (pun intended) for, say, 10 minutes. It's good for slurring because the pick (or right-hand fingers) can no longer help with projection.

With all technique-building exercises, use caution and awareness of muscle fatigue. In the end, it is not about building bulk; it is about focused power. Think of the martial artist Bruce Lee or champion boxer Manny Pacquiao.

5. TENSION

The following is a method that I designed to develop tension in music incrementally from the ground up.

Micro:

Magnifying One Harmonic Interval at a Time

Tension can be created in several ways. A common practice is "blanket" tension, whereby one plays an entire scale a half step away from the chord at hand. Obviously, that is going to give us a lot of tension since most tones are being placed outside of the chord and, yes, at this point in history, it sounds fairly obvious and uncreative.

A subtler and much more personal approach to tension is from a *gradational* standpoint: one altered note systematically added at a time. This gives us a choice as to how much tension we want at any given time while staying within the framework of the given harmony.

I've constructed charts that reflect the way I think about and hear tension, moving from the least amount to the most amount of tension. The charts are divided into three chord types: major, minor, and dominant—in this case, G Ionian, G Dorian, and G Mixolydian, or the functions of a I chord, ii chord, and V chord, respectively.

Below each of the extended gradations you will find graphs that correspond to the addition and hierarchy of tension (at least to my ears). (**Note:** I am not simply adding tension in numerical order, although it sometimes appears that way.)

Three Ways:

1. Step Gradation

Here we will add one tension note at a time while keeping the rest of the scale unaltered. This way we learn to recognize, both aurally and visually, how each altered note speaks without influence from other alterations.

G Ionian Step Gradation

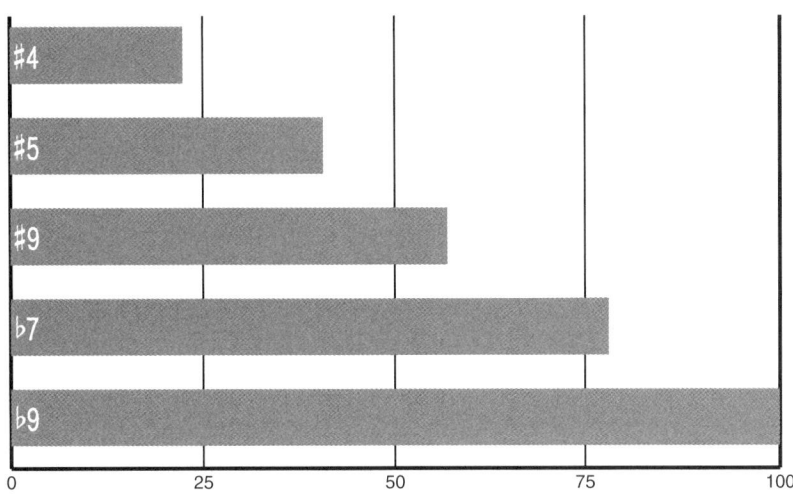

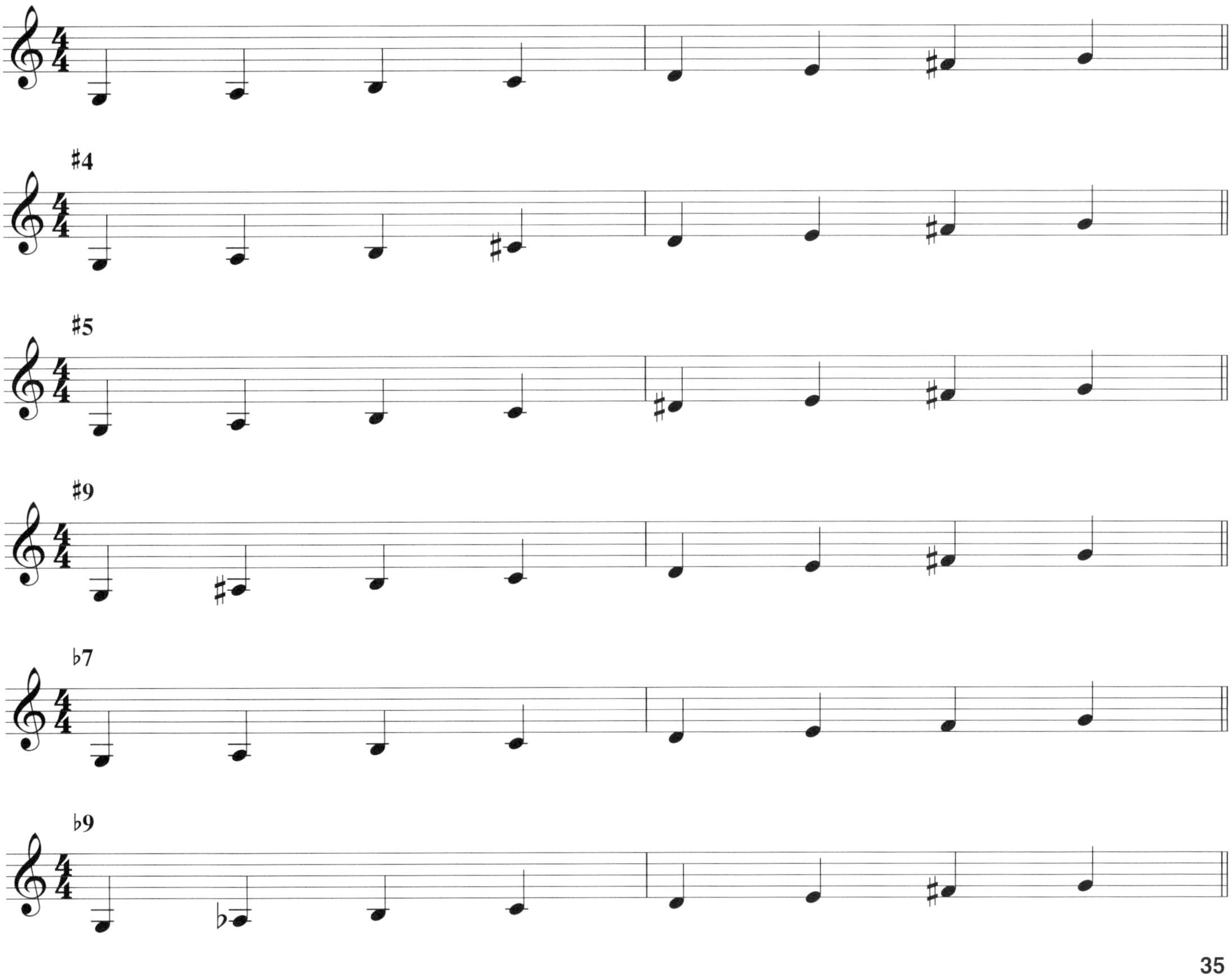

G Dorian Step Gradation

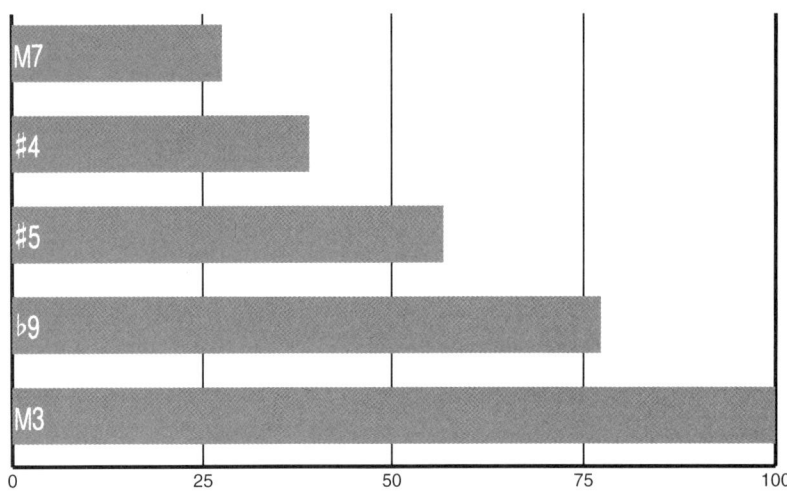

G Mixolydian Step Gradation

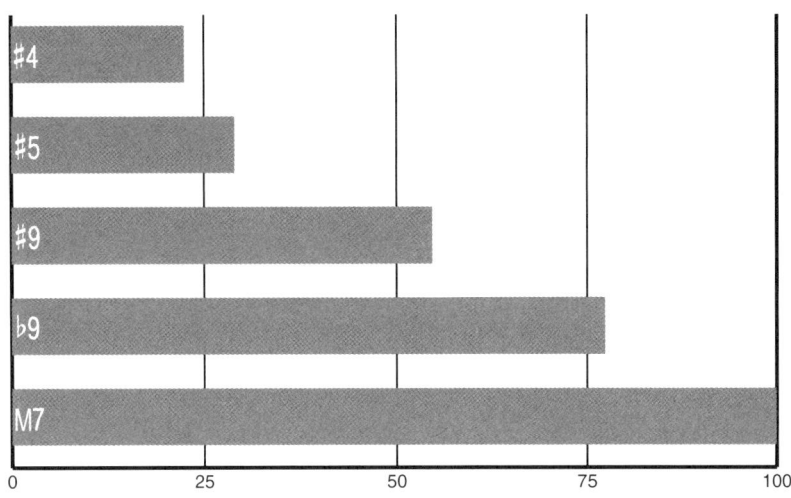

2. Full Gradation

Now we will *retain* all altered notes as we step up the ladder of alterations, adding to the chain of alterations.

G Ionian Full Gradation

G Dorian Full Gradation

G Mixolydian Full Gradation

3. Extended Gradation

When we move through tension in this manner, we can take better advantage of each specific interval. Let's say we focus on the 5th; instead of replacing our perfect 5th with the flattened or sharpened tension note, we have an option of creating more tension and interest by keeping both the altered 5ths and the perfect 5th, thereby creating a *nest of chromaticism*. These "nests," when applied to each intervallic gradation, can expand one's vocabulary and spark fresh-sounding ideas within the context of a harmonic progression. I call this "extended gradation" because, by keeping both the unaltered note and the altered note, it creates the sound of *extension*.

On the following pages are the charts that are constructed in the extended gradational format. As mentioned, I'm keeping the unaltered tones and using them in conjunction with the altered ones rather than substituting them.

Take note: When implementing *higher* tensions, we have a choice of keeping the *previous* tensions altered or unaltered while adding the new altered ones. For example; if we sharpen the 9th (assuming it is a higher tension), we can keep the previous 4th, 5th, or 6th altered or unaltered—or both. This multiplies the choices of new tension combinations significantly, as some scales will contain a perfect 5th with a ♭9th, and another version of the same scale will perhaps have a perfect 5th and a ♯5th with the ♭9th. I have circled these on all the extended gradation charts so you can see where you have a choice to alter a note (or not) as you climb the ladder of intervals. There is some crossover with intervals, such as a ♯4th sounding the same as a ♭5th, but experiment to see what combinations work best.

G Ionian Extended Gradation

G Dorian Extended Gradation

G Mixolydian Extended Gradation

Hybrid Scales

Over the years, I have become familiar with a number of Indian ragas by virtue of performing with Indian musicians. I found that many of the scales created from experimenting with this gradational approach to tension exude similar characteristics to that of the raw materials of ragas. Music is about subtlety, and one extra note makes a huge difference in aural perception. You can see (and hear) how, from just one scale, we can derive a lot of variation and therefore a large palette of sounds.

As you may have gathered, there is a mountain of material within these charts. So you won't get overwhelmed, I recommend familiarizing yourself with the content by starting with superimposing the altered notes within the framework of the unaltered scale (i.e., Step Gradation). You can then decide to mix altered notes with unaltered notes, as in Full and Extended Gradation. Eventually, choose which of these hybrid scales speak to you. By way of practice, they will eventually seep into your soloing.

The next challenge would be to make new arpeggios and random interval combinations based on your chosen scales—the same treatment you implemented when working with the basic diatonic modes.

Macro:

Bi-Tonality

A different approach to building tension is to create ideas based on the premise of *bi-tonality*, or playing two tonalities simultaneously. Bi-tonality is most often understood as a harmonic event; however, we will also use it in a melodic fashion.

Instead of smaller increments of tension, with bi-tonality, we place our focus on larger cells in order to create a wider distance between the "in" and "out"—a broader brush, if you will. The simplest way to access bi-tonality is to use triads that are diatonically incongruent, or not in the same key.

The difference between this approach and one that uses an entire scale up a half step is that, with bi-tonality, we are juxtaposing shorter increments from both inside and outside material. If we are on a G major chord, for instance, we might start an idea from a G triad and end with a B♭ triad. The latter will render the following intervals: 5th (D), ♭7th (F), and ♯9th (B♭), along with the root and major 3rd from the G triad.

Following are various examples of bi-tonality. The first juxtaposes every major triad over G major. It is advisable to call out the intervals that the superimposed triad is outlining. You can sing a G drone while playing through these or sing the triads while playing a G chord.

We can also extend the triad by adding the 9th of each. John Coltrane made this famous with his solo on "Giant Steps."

Play these triads off of G major *anchor points*. The first time, we will work only off the root. The second time, I've added B, the major 3rd of G, in order to magnify the bi-tonality within a melodic line.

Needless to say, you should play all of these in different octaves, fingerings, and configurations, as well as working them in G minor and G dominant.

"Bounce Off Notes"

There is another way to apply bi-tonality. I like to think of it as analogous to bouncing off a trampoline. This method employs target notes in a different manner. As we are playing, we would target any note in the scale, arpeggio, or line we are on and use it as a launching point (i.e., bounce off of it) to move into and imply a different tonality. It works most naturally when the targeted note is a *common tone* to both the passage you are departing from and the passage you are launching into. It can be easily applied to modal playing, but over changes, it takes a little more effort.

Track 26 **Over G Major**

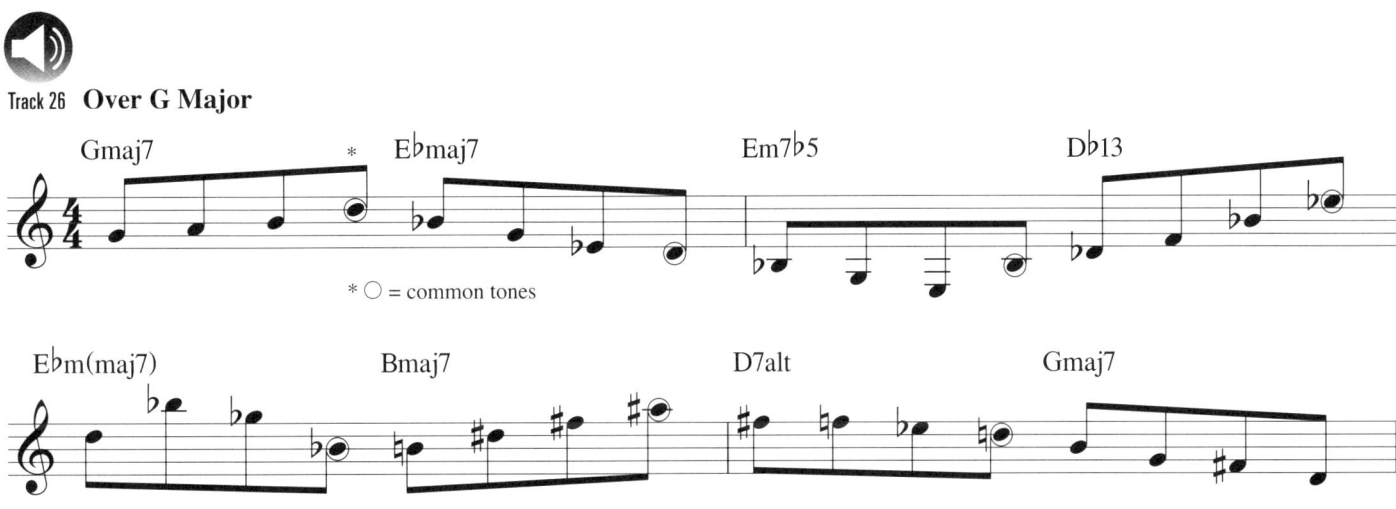

Over Changes

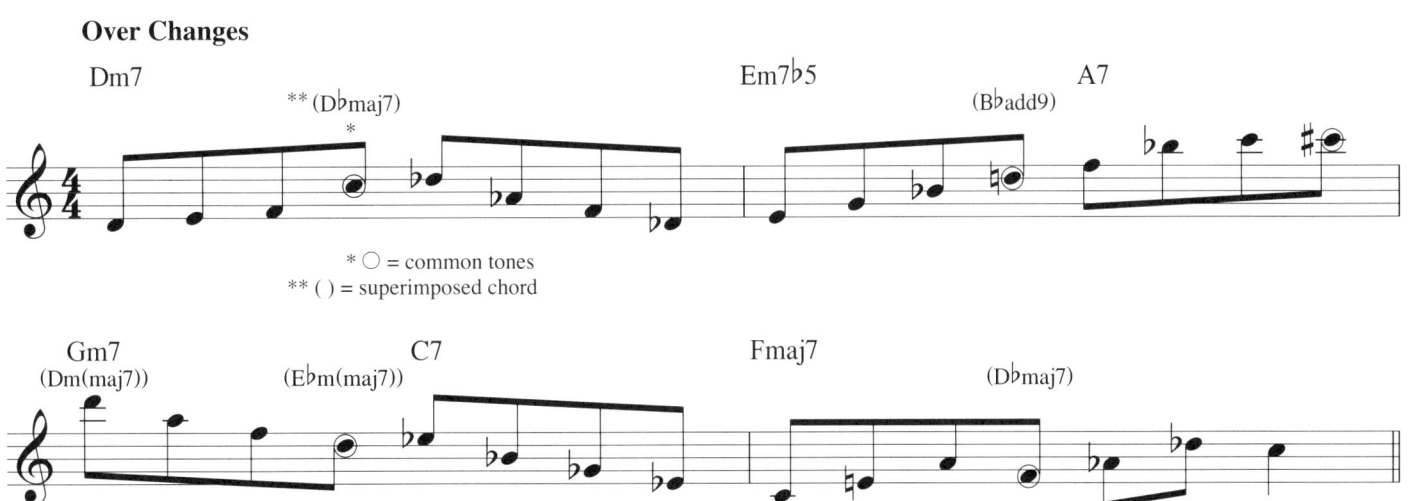

Continue "bouncing" and see where it leads you…

Arpeggios Within the Arpeggio

It is safe to say that the easier we can connect to our instrument, the quicker and the better we play. Below is a different approach to creating swift tension. By working within an arpeggio that we are well familiar with—say, Gmaj7 (G–B–D–F♯)—we can build new arpeggios off each note of that arpeggio. This gives us more possibilities right within the area of our Gmaj7 shape as we add specific tensions to the chord.

The chart below shows the procedure for Gmaj7, Gm7, and G7. And, of course, nothing is stopping you from interchanging arpeggio types: minor arpeggios over major, etc.

Over G Major

Track 27 **Harmonically**

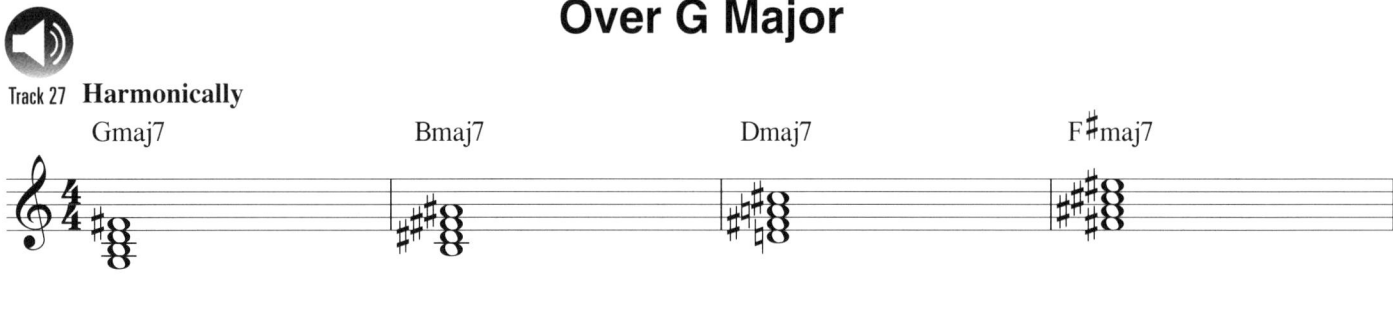

Arpeggiation

Continuous Arpeggiation

Melodically

(more chromatically)

Over G Minor

Track 28 **Harmonically**

Arpeggiation

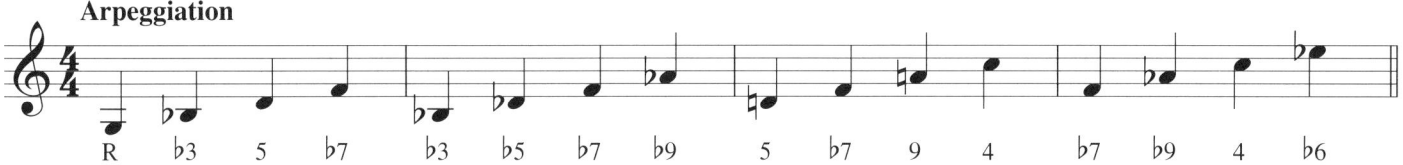

Continuous Arpeggiation

Melodically

(more chromatically)

Over G Dominant

Harmonically

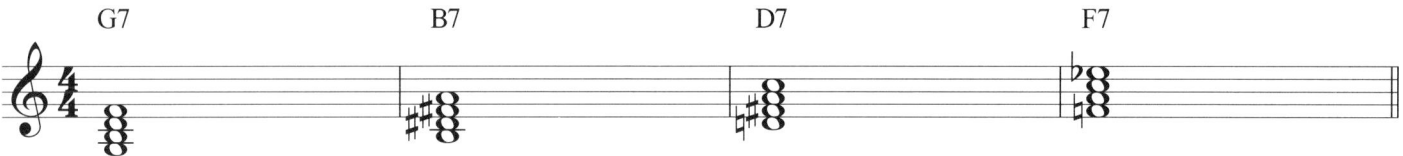

Arpeggiation

Continuous Arpeggiation

Melodically

Ways This Chapter Can Help:

- Helps us develop an overall understanding of how tension builds
- Helps us hear and play more chromatically
- Strengthens our note-targeting ability
- Trains our ears to hear more possibilities over any given chord
- Helps us develop our intimacy with unconventional sounds

EXPANDING THE BOARD

In general, the guitar lends itself to vertical playing and is probably the reason why most of us learn scales vertically. In fact, for many, it continues to be a limitation that needs attention. To counter this, a common practice is to play all scales and arpeggios on one string at a time, as this forces us to move horizontally. Another common practice is to play three-octave scales across the guitar—the Segovia method for practicing scales. Or we can use four notes per string to play scales, which forces us out of easier three-note positions. Whatever you do to explore the fretboard is going to help. Also try these:

HORIZONTAL ENGAGEMENT

The following addition to the aforementioned methods is one that helps us with the visual expansion of the fretboard, as well as the intervallic content within that expansion.

The charts below are constructed with the *black dot* representing the main tone from which intervals will be derived. You can assign any note to be the main note; for now, let's say E on the second string, fifth fret. Then play the *gray dots* on the first string as a counterpoint while simultaneously playing the E (multiple fingerings will be needed). While doing so, call out each interval you are playing.

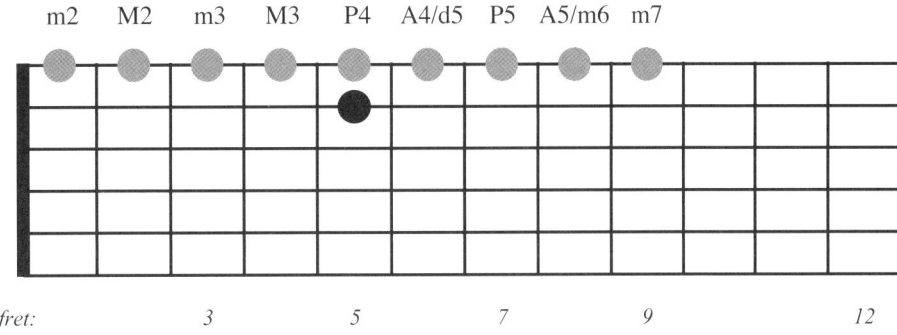

Do the same by moving the black dot to the third, fourth, fifth, and sixth strings while retaining the interval chain (gray dots) on the first string. Each time you switch the black dot, the interval makeup from the first string will change.

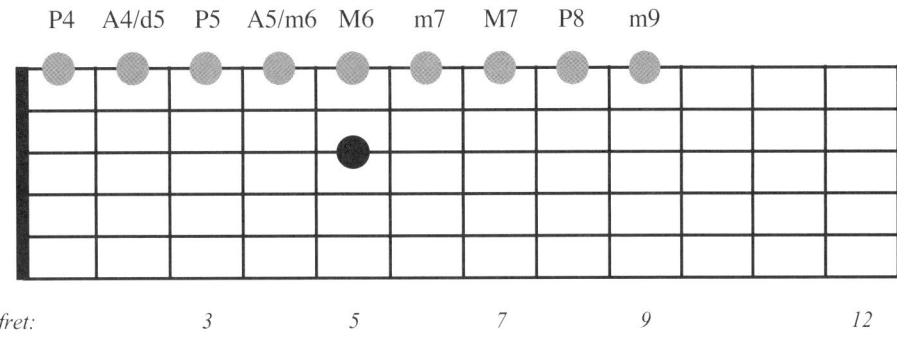

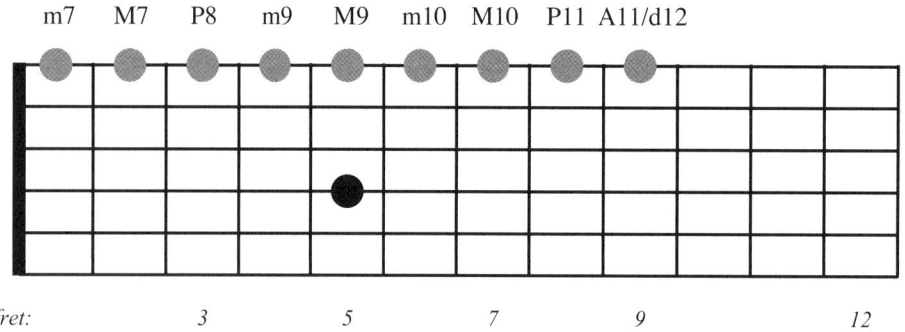

Continue to call out the intervals.

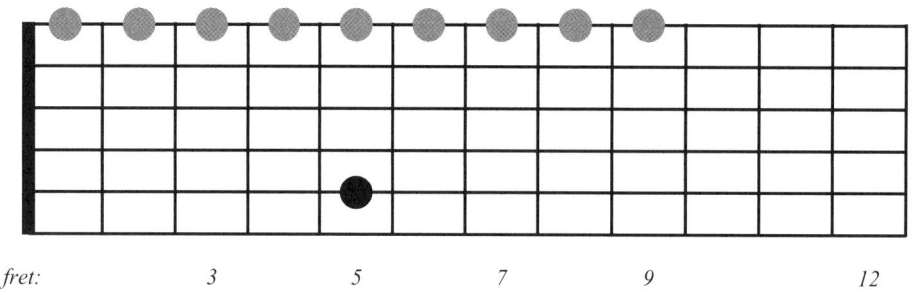

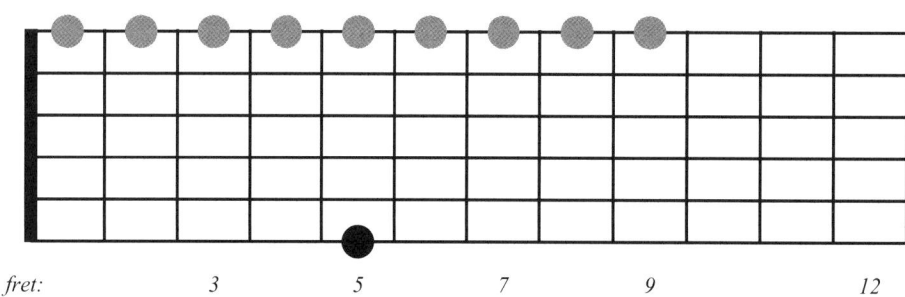

Now we'll place the interval chain on the second string and the black notes will move from the third string to the fourth, fifth, and sixth strings. Continue to move down the strings in this same fashion until you run out of strings (i.e., when the interval chain is on the fifth string and black dot is on the sixth).

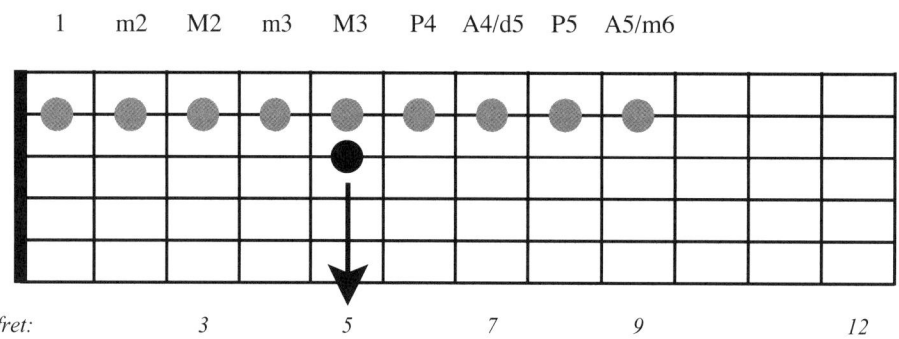

The next step is to reverse the dots (the black dot is still the main tone, however):

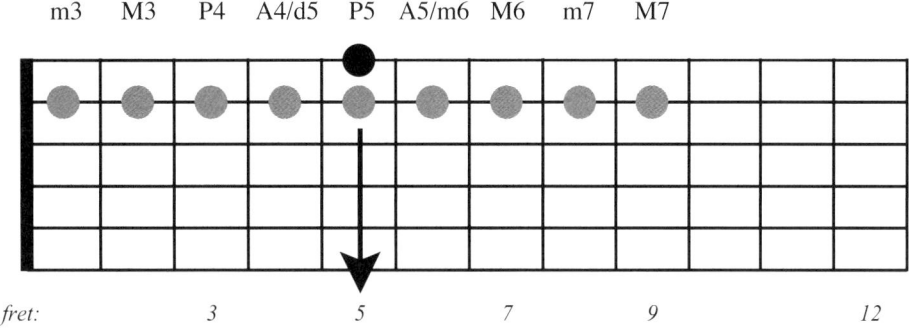

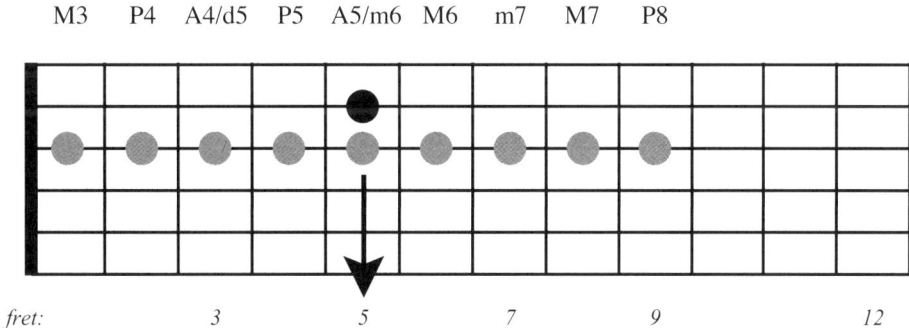

This covers a lot of territory, especially if you move it to various regions of the guitar. Try doing the whole thing every five frets.

What You Might Expect to Achieve from This:
- Improved intervallic comprehension of the fretboard
- A more natural tendency to view the guitar horizontally
- An improved ability to create counterpoint
- An improved ability to move inner voices within any chord

DISCOVERY MIRROR
(exercises for revealing deficiencies)

In order to make progress, one needs to be aware of one's deficiencies. Once you understand what areas are holding you back, only then can you directly address those areas. One of the best ways to discover such limitations is to create exercises that have an element of limitation to them.

NAVIGATION SKILLS (for horizontal playing)

Here, we narrow the "playing field"—in this case, down to string sets of three. Choose a jazz standard and move through all four sets (see below). You can start out of time, but the real test begins in time, with a metronome. We are forced to play horizontally across the fretboard and can no longer move in convenient, predetermined ways. Another benefit, particularly with the third and fourth variant, is that we begin to play and hear larger intervallic leaps.

If you find yourself stalling and looking for the next correct note in the harmony, you do not have the neck fully mastered.

String Sets:

- Sixth–Fifth–Fourth

- Third–Second–First

- Sixth–Fourth–Second

- Fifth–Third–First

TUNE IN A BOX (vertical)

After we have tested our horizontal ability, we'll work it vertically. Play over the same tune and use all strings within the zones listed below. This method can also quickly reveal your lapses within areas of the neck.

Frets: 0–5

Frets: 4–8

Frets: 7–11

Frets: 10–14

THE FOUR HORSEMEN

Many years ago, I found a weakness in my practicing. I would sometimes practice without a metronome, which is not always a bad thing, but the problem was that I would mostly choose tempo areas that were comfortable. Even though I thought they were different enough, they were along the same lines.

Once I made that discovery, I decided to take a larger approach and devise a spectrum of tempos that would instantly reflect my weakness—if, indeed, I were out of shape. You might need to work a few tempos before you find your spectrum, but mine is as follows:

- 70–80bpm

- 100bpm

- 120bpm

- 140–150bpm

I use this in two ways: I play each tempo in quarter notes (i.e., one quarter note for every metronome beep), then I play each tempo in double time so that each beep of the metronome lands on beats 2 and 4. This works the jazz feel more, as if a drummer is playing the hi-hat on the backbeat.

I occasionally practice in 60 or 160 bpm, but those tempos are what I like to call "fringe" tempos. If there is a specific tune I'm learning that calls for one, then I'll practice it. For the most part, these four areas cover a broad range of issues for me. As an example, playing constant eighth-note triplets in double time at 100bpm over harmony is not effortless for me. I know I will be out of shape for a gig if I cannot do that at home.

COMPOSITIONAL PLAYING

Compositional playing starts with the willingness not to rely on predetermined patterns or licks as the means to an end. Although we learn by directly repeating melodic structures, in my judgment, if not watchful, they can become hindrances to our ability to tell a story. Memorized patterns can often come off sounding preconceived, not in the moment, and not very imaginative, especially when used in solo after solo.

Compositional playing, on the other hand, is based on *motivic development* and is what most often creates truly memorable solos. Developing a melodic idea is essential in telling a musical story, but since we do not use words when soloing, *meaning* can become indirect and subjective. That is precisely why we need to cultivate and work on the time-tested compositional methods used by masters in classical and jazz music.

CALL/RESPONSE/ECHO

Call and response is perhaps the most common and essential compositional device we can implement. It is as simple as responding to a statement with a "reflecting" statement. Below is a simple example of this principle in action. The initial statement we make is the "call"; it's our "golden nugget." Regardless of how great it really is, since it's your first statement, it will be what the listener (and band) will hold on to, albeit subconsciously. What naturally follows is a "response"—a melodic statement that mimics the character of the call but also extends it. The response can be simple or complex but should retain the original *feeling* of the call. It can be as simple as changing one or two intervals, moving in the same direction, or retaining only the rhythm—if, indeed, the rhythm conveys character (constant eighth notes are not going to carry enough character, but a tune like "Autumn Leaves," for instance, will).

Track 30 **Call**

Response

It is important to remember that we are focusing on the initial "vibe" in the call and following that up with an extension—the response to that vibe. It is not about over-analyzing; however, it is often the case that a response does share many similar aspects with its call. This is exactly the reason why it is important to exercise our intuitive muscle by slowing things down and analyzing so that eventually we hear and feel what is behind the intervallic/rhythmic/textural makeup, in a variety of tempos. In this sense, you should be able to see and hear some commonality between the two phrases.

The previous example showed us a basic call and response. The next, and slightly more difficult, step is to create an *echo*. What this essentially means is that we now start moving further away from our initial idea while still retaining some of its character. This is very subjective, and therefore we need to rely on our intuition.

compositional playing

Below, I have added an echo. The test of continuity comes full circle when you place the initial call at the very end and see if it shares the character of the echo. If it does not, then you've lost the character of the call and may want to change something to "bring it home."

Track 31 **Call**

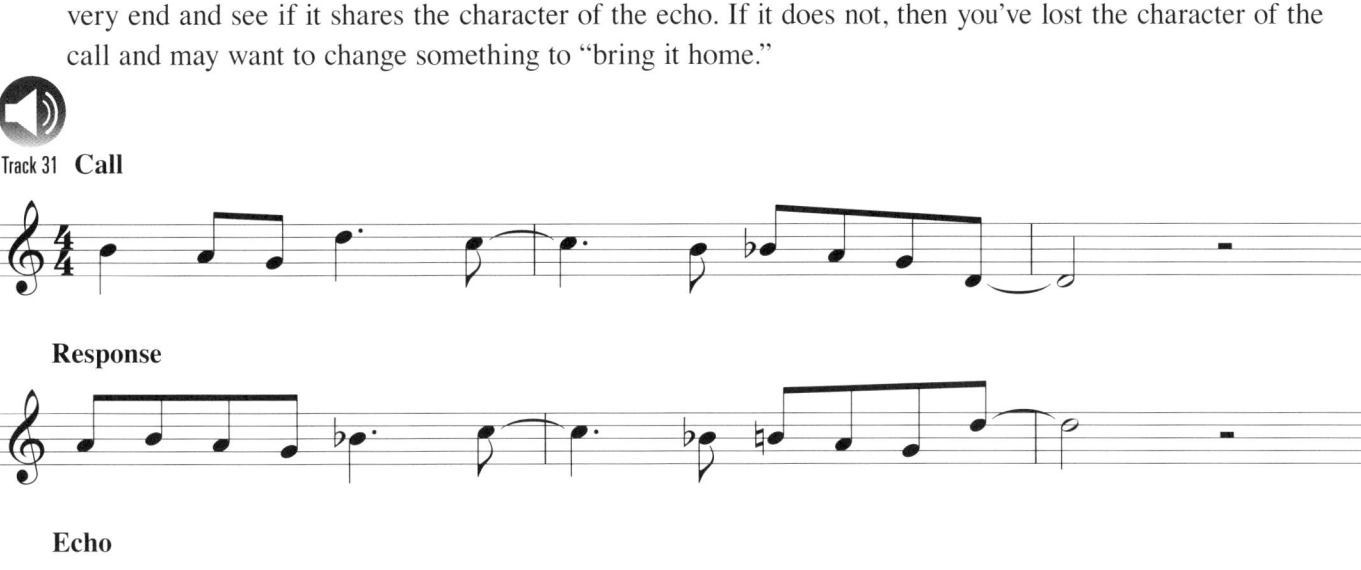

Here it is on a few bars of "Stella":

Track 32 **Call**   **Response**

Echo

Echo 2   **Echo 3**

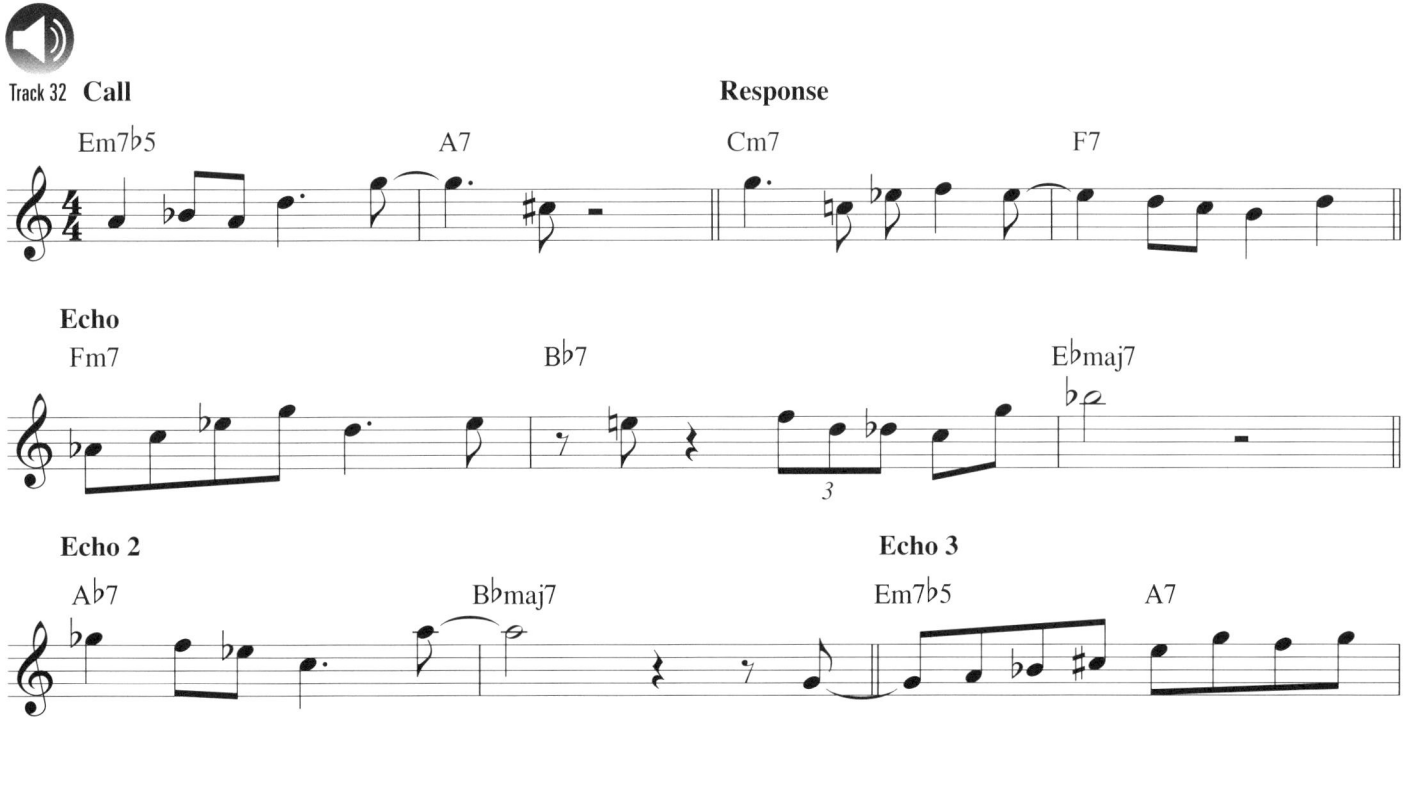

Building more echoes on the initial echo is another step. It is tricky because we do not want the process to sound rigid or mechanical but do want things to flow naturally. Again, practicing and writing out ideas and using your discretion with this method will help you engrain it and make stronger and longer statements. It will help you tell a *musical story*.

Now use this call to write out your own response and echo:

CHARACTER

As mentioned, the initial statement in a solo is powerful and, in order to tell a musical story, whatever one plays afterwards should be related to it. Furthermore, the ability to compositionally develop a melody is often determined by the strength of the initial statement. What is it that makes a melody come across sounding like a strong statement? This is a question I have asked myself and remind myself to revisit on occasion. The essential answer for me is *character*—that is, good music has plenty of it. Even if it is music I'd rather not listen to, if it contains a semblance of character, I can appreciate its merit.

compositional playing

What is character made up of? That is a more complex question with a subjective answer, but I do think there is an objective take on it. First, what it is not necessarily made up of is the lowest common denominator—a scale, arpeggio, or pattern. We create character from these tools by the way we handle them, but in their essence, they are raw materials with little meaning. The larger question is: what do we bring to these materials and how do we give them a voice without sounding like we are "using" them? This seems to be what great soloists are able to do.

By and large, character is born from how we approach a passage of music, as well as the passage of music itself. A perfect exhibition comes from the one and only Charlie Parker. Below is one chorus of blues from Parker's "Au Privave" solo (and the first jazz solo I learned). When you play through this chorus, you may notice how it instantly possesses character. Are there particular areas within the lines that give them and the solo radiance, like the interval or chromatic choices? Can you find the call, response, and echo in this chorus? Somehow, it is engineered in a way that speaks to us almost universally—as if not a single note can be changed without ruining the entire feeling (think Bach). This phrase contains so much even without hearing the source (Charlie Parker). If you listen to him play it, you will hear how the worlds of substance and subject join forces—that is, character of idea combining with character of player. This is the optimal combination!

Track 33 **Au Privave**

COMPOSITIONAL VARIATION AND APPLICATIONS

Compositional variation is an indispensable, structured method that helps us make the most out of a single melodic idea. It can also help to create response and echo. As with everything, it is beneficial to see things both on and off the guitar, so before playing through the variations and actually hearing them, take a look and get a feel for what is happening visually. Starting from the basic cell—in this case, a passage on "Giant Steps"—we can easily see that, based on the shape of the music notation alone, there is a lot of musical variation to be found within the initial cell. By simply applying directives, we can create remarkably new takes on the original cell while retaining its character.

Here, I progress from least aggressive to most aggressive variation.

- **Octave Displacement** is as simple as taking one note and changing its octave. This example takes the second note of each phrase and shifts it down an octave. You can also shift it up an octave.

- **Diminution** means to reduce. In this case, I've reduced the length of three eighth notes to an eighth-note triplet, which then made room to lengthen the remaining note.

- **Fragmenting** makes use of rests in order to create new phraseology. By replacing a note with a rest, we gain a powerfully different feel and rhythmical bounce.

- **Retrograde** means to reverse. The phrase starts from its last note and ends with its first note.

- **Double Octave Displacement** is changing octaves for two notes. This starts to create a wilder sound, especially if you vary your choices. I've also done a variation on the variation.

- **Extension** can be a number of things. In this case, I simply added a passing tone or chromatic tone for the purpose of creating a more active line. You can also employ more 16th notes to extend the line further.

- **Permutation** is a way to expand the line while also moving further away from the character. Here, I've changed the two inner notes (beats 1 and 2). This was done because I wanted to retain some of the original content while moving away from it, which is accomplished with great effect when we bookend the original notes as we digress and come back.

Try putting these to the test by applying them to one of your ideas.

BREAKING OUT OF HABITUAL PLAYING

Here are some ideas that have helped me break out of old phrases that I find myself repeating. It will be beneficial to slow down and use this information either out of time or on ballad-like tempos at first. We are essentially breaking down routine muscle-memory patterns that have been created over time and so we need to unravel those knots slowly.

PLAYING STANDARDS IN ODD METERS

This may sound simple in concept, but the idea behind it is that your "catch phrases" are probably based in 4/4 or 3/4. Therefore, when you play a standard in 5/4, 7/4, 9/4, 5/8, 7/8, or 9/8, it forces you to come up with new ideas based on duration of the bar—you no longer can play the lines that fit so well in 4/4 or 3/4 that most standards are written in. This one can be done in any tempo.

START ON THE OPPOSITE BEAT

If you find yourself playing a lot of the same lines, it is assumed that you are comfortable playing them. That comfort might come from the fact that you are always playing them from a particular beat. Try starting those lines from the opposite beat (i.e., either a downbeat or an upbeat).

DOUBLING NOTES

Take any stock line and simply repeat one of the notes in the line. Doing so is usually enough to make it sound different. Try it on a simple triad first and you may notice it sounds like you're playing more than a simple triad.

REPLACE ANY NOTE

This is an obvious one but very effective. Again, it makes the line sound considerably different simply by changing one note.

EMPLOY COMPOSITIONAL VARIATION

Apply compositional variation to one line. It's a more extensive process but you will have much more to work with.

LAUNCH PHRASES

I sometimes use a few short, memorized phrases in order to launch into more spontaneous ideas. For instance, the 1, 3, and 5 of any triad (I like triads because they feel grounded, both physically and musically) or a combination of any 3–4 notes that feels grounded. This becomes a reference point for new ideas to launch from and ultimately conflates our ideas in varying ways. I like to launch from the lower strings and move into the top strings for the new ideas, but we can launch from the top strings, as well.

VARYING LINE LENGTH

Break up a line into two or three parts and add notes in between the parts. Not only will your lines lengthen, but now you can switch the parts of the line. If you repeat a part or add new notes in between, that gives you a lot more vocabulary to work with from the one line.

CHAIN-LINKING (nonstop eighth notes)

This is not an official term, but it essentially means using only eighth notes to play a solo on a tune. In this manner, our lines do not breathe and we are forced to keep up with the continuous eighths. It is challenging to make a musical statement while doing this, but for now, we are trying to find new pathways on the guitar, albeit by force. A metronome is recommended, as it drives the momentum. You can also use constant triplets or 16ths. If the harmony is complex, you will soon find areas on the guitar that are more challenging, and that is the point.

LEFT-HAND COMBINATIONS

1–2–3, 2–3–4, 1–2–4, and 1–3–4: limiting your left-hand combinations is very challenging because you will realize immediately that you cannot depend on memorized ideas. Playing with these finger combinations almost forces you to think and play more melodically. For instance, try to play your favorite arpeggio, using only the 2–3–4 combination.

I hope this will encourage you to come up with other ways to break out of habitual playing.

PRACTICE METHODS

To play consistently, sometimes we need to engage in methods of practice that may, at first, seem unrelated to making good music but, in retrospect, make perfect sense. Just as professional athletes use unconventional practice methods that serve to strengthen their performance, we also need to practice the mechanics behind playing consistently strong. Needless to say, it will vary for most players, but below are some suggestions until you refine your own system.

SHOCK PRACTICING

High-Action Guitar

Often, one of my guitars will be slightly "out of whack," but rather than adjusting it, I like to work with the "off" action. Essentially, this takes me out of my comfort zone; I will try to make music and create the flow I am accustomed to having but with a guitar action I'm not used to. At first, my rhythm will be out of sync due to technical constraints, and this is the point—to work around the hindrances in order to come close to my normal musical abilities. This actually helps me to be better prepared when playing in a live situation because things are rarely copasetic at the gig (bad amp, stage is too small, etc.). If you are always comfortable practicing at home, how are you going to adjust quickly when you get on the gig, where conditions are rarely as comfortable?

Practicing to Loudness

Another way to get "shocked" is to practice to loud music. This is often more realistic than practicing to silence or a metronome and provides us with a simulation of playing with a band. It tries your chops like nothing else at home can. Crank up a tune on the stereo and play with it.

Use a New Scale While Playing in an Odd Meter

This combination is especially tough because we are combining two uncomfortable areas and dealing with them simultaneously. So, if it's not the Dorian mode in 5/4 that is pulling at your mental strings, practice in 11/8 with the harmonic major scale, for instance. What you may notice is that an unfamiliar scale within an unfamiliar meter imposes more mental weight than you are used to. This seems to imply that we are working a side of the brain that is less developed… at least that's how it feels to me!

The objective is to be uncomfortable and yet pull things off musically.

SOLOING ALONE (with a bass player in mind)

While practicing alone on a tune, many of us tend to resolve phrases on strong notes such as the root, 3rd, or 5th in order to consciously (or unconsciously) feel musically complete. Consistently practicing this way often leads us to do the same when playing with a band. It can be musically limiting, especially if there is a bass player in the group, because resolutions become less colorful, as you may be resolving tension in a similar fashion as the bass.

Practicing on tunes with a bass player in mind can be a good way to not fall into this trap. This way, we are more likely to resolve on a 7th, ♯4th, or 13th, for instance, rather than the more solid root, 3rd, or 5th.

SOLOING ALONE (with a drummer in mind)

Another tendency when practicing soloing alone is that we might end up rhythmically resolving on downbeats as a place of security. It is a grounded feeling similar to resolving on the root, 3rd, or 5th of a chord. Here, an imaginary drummer helps us to become aware of the beat(s). Try finishing your phrases earlier than you usually would and just let the pulse (drummer) carry the weight of the music. Or try ending after the downbeat. When you do play with a band, you will find more comfort in letting the drummer (or others) fill up the space you left, which often results in better interaction and communication anyway.

USING THE TELEVISION

This seems counter to good practicing, of course, and it usually is. Having said that, some days when I am just not inspired to focus, yet I do need to prepare my chops, I will use the TV in a couple of ways.

First, I usually play an electric guitar acoustically, so in order to hear myself over the sound of the TV, I'll need to play a little harder. That can help build muscles and projection. Second, I will sometimes play with a metronome, and when theme songs or commercials come on, I'll try to maintain my metronome's tempo over whatever is coming from the jingle. That can be a challenge that is not found in my usual practice regiment. Third, I'll use the jingles for ear training simply by trying to quickly find the tonality and learn the melody of a jingle in one attempt.

Again, this is a little respite from *true* practicing.

IDEAS TO CONSIDER

TECHNIQUE VS. VOCABULARY

I am often asked about technique—particularly how to play fast. The problem with posing such a question is that it leaves out the other more important half of the equation: the *content*. Better questions that might be posed are: What is being expressed behind and beyond the technique? Or, what purpose does technique serve?

From time to time, a technical exercise can help us strengthen our hands by building the subtle muscles we directly use in our particular way of playing but, ultimately, technique is only useful in application of musical content. In this sense, I'll pose another question: What are you doing to work on your vocabulary?

Essentially, I am advocating not to spend too much time on technical exercises, as some players do, but rather spend time on creating a flow that directly stems from vocabulary, new or old. If you are looking for "more chops," for instance, you should come up with more technically challenging lines and then work the technique within those ideas in various tempos. This way, we are instilling in our subconscious minds that there is a reason for technique and that it is being applied to make music rather than running exercises solely based on flash or muscle (other than warming up).

TIMING VS. TARGETING

The guitar is a visual instrument. The time we spend applying the tools of music to the guitar are very much linked with our visual sense. This can work for us or against us.

It works *for* us because we can simultaneously hear and see through chord changes—visually targeting notes inside or outside of the scale or harmony. While practicing, we can experiment at great lengths, searching for new notes and ideas that we may not hear at first, but through the visual process, we can train our ears to eventually hear them. In this sense, we have two guiding approaches: hearing then seeing, and vice versa. The former is how we usually learn—we transcribe or hear an idea and then transfer it to the guitar with multiple fingerings (i.e., multiple visuals). The latter is using the visual to target areas outside of our normal inner vocabulary. Both approaches eventually can work in tandem while we are in the process of playing.

However, the way this visual aspect can work *against* us is when it takes precedence, which then leads to undesirable results: rushing or dragging while trying to outline the changes or target that interesting note; not following up on our ideas due to a reliance on patterns. In other words, rhythmically, our visual sense is not always aligned with the pulse, so we rush or drag according to it; melodically, the visual is not always in *character* with our proceeding ideas, so we play disjointedly.

One way to remedy the habit of *rhythmic non-alignment* while playing through harmony is to do the following: choose a tune that contains challenging harmony, at a tempo that is uncomfortable (probably an up-tempo). Complex harmony that demands constant resolution in order to outline the moving chords, played at an uncomfortable tempo, forces us to make quick adjustments; consequently, we are more likely to rush or drag.

Begin to solo over the tune as you normally would but purposefully end your phrases in two manners: 1) just before every chord change, and 2) just before finishing each eighth-note triplet or 16th-note line. By doing so, you will be exercising your *reactionary* muscle and therefore more likely to have control of the time/pocket, as opposed to being overly influenced by visual "target resolutions." It can also sound more interesting!

ideas to consider

Below are musical examples for each, and the second one is demonstrated on the audio track.

Track 35   **1. Ending phrase just before every chord change**

Track 36   **2. Ending phrase just before each eighth-note triplet or 16th-note line**

While soloing, I can see a lot of melodic choices on the guitar because, as mentioned, guitarists often apply musical ideas visually. By doing the aforementioned exercises, I am once again telling my subconscious mind not to jump at melodic or rhythmical ideas and target notes in a reactionary, rushed manner, simply because I'm going for a resolution. Furthermore, I found that the best way not to get caught up in the lure of the visual is to remind myself to listen to what I just played (along with listening to the band). By doing so, I develop my melodic ideas more naturally.

Sometimes it is more musically gratifying *not* to end your phrases... not to resolve what you are seeing, hearing, or thinking. It worked well for Miles Davis!

TOOLS VS. END RESULT

It is important to remember that scales, arpeggios, patterns, and intervals are what constitute the tools of music, but they are not the end result of music. It becomes apparent to me when a soloist is leaning on tools to get through a solo versus having command over creating a musical statement. Outlining the chord changes, for instance, is not a means to an end but rather something we master through practice in order to focus on music-making while playing. It takes a competent and mature player to refrain from settling on the tools and replacing that with creating and improvising a statement. Of course, it's not an all-or-nothing situation; arpeggios and scales can be applied to a solo directly and can work within your musical statement, but having the choice to do that rather than not having a choice is what I'm speaking about.

Again, experiment by choosing a difficult tune from a fake book and set the metronome to a challenging tempo. Can you play the tune in a "melodic" fashion without sounding like you're depending on arpeggios, scales, or patterns to get you through the solo?

At the end of the day, after we internalize whatever it is we are working on, it is important to separate oneself from the "sound" of practicing.

HEARING/FEELING VS. THINKING/CALCULATING

Students often complain about practicing new material only to have it seemingly never surface when they are improvising. We obviously want new materials to surface in our playing, or else why practice them? But forcing any material to make an appearance in a playing situation often comes out sounding awkward and unnatural.

A good way to introduce new ideas into your playing—whether it is a line, chord, or rhythm—is to revisit each multiple times a day. Literally take one minute for each new thing, three times a day. By doing so, we bake them into our minds and no longer need to think of them while improvising.

An additional step is to relate the new ideas to previously memorized ideas, linking them to one another. If it is a new minor line, then play it just after another one you know well. The only thing I personally would not do is to relate the new ideas to a specific tune. If you do so, you may be foisting specific variables of the tune on said ideas and thus *limiting* their usage to that tune or tunes of the same nature.

JAZZ AND AWARENESS

In my estimation, focused awareness is the most vital "non-music" tool for us to cultivate in order to make music, and even more so, jazz music. Playing with other musicians who are communicating by shifting their ideas to either gravitate towards yours or challenge yours with new content, continuously, is not found in any music I know of other than jazz. High-caliber communication also permeates classical Indian music, Cuban music, funk, and many others, no doubt, but it is of a different nature than jazz.

All this is to say: any form of music that simultaneously expects from its participants a combination of improvised expression and collective communication is inherently challenging. The more the music is centered on this principle, the more focused awareness helps us to connect with the musical layers. Just try to remember how it felt to play a rock/pop tune in a band versus a standard with a trio or quartet. Which one was looser and needed more attention to form, downbeats, harmony, melodic and rhythmic variation, etc., all the while being shaped by other members' spontaneous and surprising musical choices?

Most of us have had moments of playing when we are in a simple state of mind, communicating our musical ideas while reflecting off of the band—moments that capture the spirit of jazz music. Unfortunately, all too often, we are caught up in our "limited" mental mindset; we are either stumbling on the tools of the craft, annoyed with our sound, wondering what people think, or we are playing so well that we get caught up listening to and admiring ourselves, dismissing the band! While it is necessary to address important factors such as knowing the music, our sound, etc., it's unnecessary to get caught up in the lesser inducements that are vying for our attention. Doing so creates a separation from the whole. This is why it is important to remind ourselves periodically to focus on collectivity, which brings us to awareness.

Awareness is the larger door we want to open when playing with a group. I view focus a little differently than awareness. In my interpretation, focus heightens attention towards a specific thing, akin to a flashlight. Awareness, although its backbone is focus, encompasses one's full spectrum of surroundings, much like a floodlight. Heightening awareness intensifies collectivity simply because we are not caught up on separate components that are within our own experience, but rather we are placing focus on the middle of the stage; we hear and play from the middle out, not from one of the side speakers. We can view this as focused awareness.

> **Focused awareness can be practiced like anything else.**

Focused awareness can be practiced like anything else. Try the following and see what results come up for you.

Before starting your practice session, sit comfortably with your guitar in hand. With closed eyes, simply focus on your breath. This will prepare you to get into the required space. After a few minutes, or when you truly feel like you have connected with your breath, slowly guide your attention towards whatever sounds are around you in that moment, regardless of how subtle they are.

Now continue to focus, but on all sounds simultaneously. Take note of whatever there is without trying to separate, question, or define it. After you've felt a *oneness* with your surroundings, bring attention back to your breath while including the full scope of stimuli. The breath now functions like the guitar, as it is given attention without closing the door to all else. It is a balancing act with multiple stimuli calling for your attention—similar to playing jazz and akin to hearing from the middle out. You can interchange between only focusing on the breath, to cultivating awareness of both the breath and surrounding sounds. This trains the brain to place focus anywhere at anytime, the foundation of meditation. Whether we are in tune with one thing or the collectivity of many becoming one, it is focus that is a prerequisite.

Now we know how it feels to be engaged in both singular focus and inclusive focus. We know how not to limit our field of focus on listening to one component—usually our playing—and instead, to place it on the oneness of our surrounding environment. In this sense, we are less likely to play too loud, over comp, and be unaffected by others, and more likely to listen to all, blend, and make a collective statement.

Ideally, and after we have practiced enough of the raw materials on the guitar, this paradigm positions us in a space of truly becoming the witness of our playing situation. The witness need not be caught up in *over-thinking*, which usually leads to separation, but in being engaged by and through collective listening. Our musical choices now hinge more on intuition, and we know scientifically that intuition takes place before thought. The music should be all that is left.

Track 37

To close out the book, here is my sample improvisation over a chorus of "Stella by Starlight," incorporating some of the concepts we've explored.

RECOMMENDED BOOKS

Beethoven: His Life and Music by Jeremy Siepmann

Thelonious Monk: The Life and Times of an American Original by Robin D.G. Kelley

Coltrane on Coltrane: The John Coltrane Interviews by Chris Devito

The Fighter's Mind: Inside the Mental Game by Sam Sheridan

Zen Tennis: Playing in the Zone by Dr. Joseph Parent

The Raga Guide by Joep Bor

Joys and Sorrows: Reflections by Pablo Casals by Albert E. Kahn

Julian Bream: A Life on the Road by Tony Palmer

Effortless Mastery by Kenny Werner

Awakening Kundalini: The Path to Radical Freedom by Dr. Lawrence Edwards

ACKNOWLEDGMENTS

I would like to thank the many important teachers I've spent time with, short and long term: Paul La Rose, Joe Diorio, Peter Sprague, Ted Greene, Kenny Werner, John Abercrombie, Vince Mendoza, Rodney Jones, Terry Plumeri, Duke Miller, Les Wise, Edgar Grana, Harihar Rao, Ray Spiegel, Ustad Alla Rakha, Scott Tennant, Lenny Breau, Milcho Leviev, Jack Wilkins, Rich DeRosa, Steve Watson, and Barry Kermisch.

I would also like to thank the following for enlightening my musical path: Kiran Ahluwalia, Rudresh Mahanthappa, Ted Makler, Dave Phillips, Tom Chang, Dan Weiss, Nitin Mitta, Lon M. Teller, Anton Machleder, Ahmad Mansour, among others.

Thanks to the following for continued encouragement: Abdul, Feroza, and Robert Abbasi, Jagjit, Dolly, and Kiran Ahluwalia, and my friends!

Thanks to the following for their initial encouragement and feedback on the book: Joe Diorio, Les Wise, Ted Makler, Kiran Ahluwalia, George Matthew Jr., Anand Krishnamurthy, Ryan-Imran Husain, and Adam Small.

Thanks to Kurt Plahna, Jeff Schroedl, and all at Hal Leonard.

ABOUT THE AUTHOR

Voted #1 "Rising-Star Guitarist" in 2013's *DownBeat* Critics Poll and successively placed in the top-ten guitarists alongside John Scofield and Pat Metheny, guitarist and composer Rez Abbasi is considered one of the foremost versatile modern jazz guitar players the world over.

Making New York home for the past 25 years, Abbasi has created a unique sound that is stimulated by his jazz pedigree and South Asian-American upbringing. He earned his Bachelor of Music from the Manhattan School of Music, released 13 albums to date, has been featured on many recordings, and has garnered multiple composition commissions. Abbasi also conducts clinics worldwide.

For more information, please visit: *www.RezTone.com*.

DISCOGRAPHY

Third Ear (1995)

Modern Memory (1998)

Out of Body (2002)

Snake Charmer (2005)

Bazaar (2007)

Things to Come (2009)

Natural Selection (2010)

Suno Suno (2011)

Continuous Beat (2013)

Intents & Purposes (2015)

Behind the Vibration (2016)

Unfiltered Universe (2017)

A Throw of Dice - Film Score (2018)